Persuade
IN A MINUTE

Tony Wrighton is an NLP (Neuro-Linguistic Programming) Trainer and Master Practitioner. His self-development audio-books have sold over 100,000 copies and have been Top 10 bestsellers on iTunes in many countries around the world. In addition to his work as a coach, Tony has worked as a TV and radio presenter for fifteen years.

www.tonywrighton.com

Persuade
IN A MINUTE

10 STEPS TO
GETTING YOUR WAY

Tony Wrighton

2 4 6 8 10 9 7 5 3 1

Published in 2011 by Virgin Books, an imprint of Ebury Publishing
A Random House Group Company

The Random House Group Limited Reg. No. 954009

Addresses for companies within the Random House Group can be found at
www.randomhouse.co.uk

A CIP catalogue record for this book is available from the British Library

The Random House Group Limited supports the Forest Stewardship Council®
(FSC®), the leading international forest certification organisation.
All our titles that are printed on Greenpeace-approved FSC® certified
paper carry the FSC® logo. Our paper procurement policy can be found
at www.randomhouse.co.uk/environment

Printed in the UK by CPI Bookmarque, Croydon, CR0 4TD

ISBN 9780753522561

To buy books by your favourite authors and register for offers, visit
www.randomhouse.co.uk

Contents

Introduction »

Welcome to *Persuade in a Minute*. Every technique in this book takes a minute or less. That's all it takes to start being more persuasive and get others thinking about a 'yes' instead of a 'no'.

You don't have to read the book cover to cover. Simply start reading right now at any area where you think you might want to be more persuasive. Some of the techniques are serious, some are great fun, and they all work towards ensuring people become more receptive to your message.

You'll find a number of specific ways to approach each situation. By all means use them, but don't think they are the only way. If you find something else that works better, then use that instead. And be sceptical. In fact, the more sceptical you are, the better. Don't assume everything works, but instead give it all a go and see what works best for you.

Finally, a brief word about the importance of doing stuff for the right reasons. When you genuinely believe that something is 'right' for the other person, you're then persuading them for the best of reasons, and you have a much better chance of hearing that magic word. 'Yes'.

CHAPTER 1

Three magic shortcuts to get you started

Karen runs a gym in central London. She wants to persuade more of the lovely people who come in to use the gym once or twice a week to sign up for personal training with her. She gets on very well with everybody, but people seem to prefer a casual five-minute chat with her to actually booking a proper session.

In addition, a lot of the gym members seem to come in, spend half an hour talking to friends, watching the monitors and walking around filling their water bottles and then go home having done very little. She knows many of them would like to lose weight or tone up, but she notices that it often just doesn't happen. She wants to help them. Plus, of course, she would love the extra income that would come from having more private clients.

She knows it costs quite a lot for private sessions, but she passionately believes that it's a good thing for everybody when they sign up.

Let's start by making you more persuasive straight away. Coming up, you'll find three general ways that you can make people more receptive to your message. Use them all. See which ones work best. And have fun with them. The three shortcuts are:

▶▶ *The Magic Touch*
▶▶ *Changing position*
▶▶ *The most persuasive word in the world?*

The Magic Touch

Nicolas Gueguen is a persuasion expert who clearly enjoys his work. He's done lots of fun studies, including whether make-up on women is more likely to attract men and, my personal favourite: 'Bust Size and Hitchhiking: A Field Study'. Seriously. Can you guess what the results were?

Anyway, another of his studies was based in a small bar in a market town on the Atlantic coast of France. He and his co-researcher, Celine Jacob, discovered there that one single instant act of body language could dramatically increase the amount of tips a waitress received.

Once a customer was seated, the waitress would come over, smile, and ask them what they wanted to drink. She would then bring the drink over, and the bill. After the customer had left, she would return to the table to clear it, carefully noting if she'd been left a tip and how much it was.

However, with half the customers, the waitress had an instruction to briefly touch their forearm just once during the initial meeting when the order was being taken. When this single initial touch had been made, the chance of the customer leaving a tip increased by 128 per cent.

The researchers found that a touch creates an unspoken, unconsciously remembered bond between two people.

So how can you use the Magic Touch to make deals? Help you succeed? Attract somebody? Get what you want? After all, the waitress only touches the customer when first taking the order, not when actually bringing the bill. The unconscious mind seems to notice and file away the Magic Touch, and can act on it even after a period of time has passed.

And the connection between touch and persuasion has been recorded not just in the waitress experiment but in numerous studies elsewhere. For instance, it was found that a brief touch increased the answer rate to a street survey. And customers who were briefly touched by an employee when entering a shop increased the amount of time they spent in there, as well as the amount of money.

Be careful where you touch. According to the Gueguen study, it has to be specifically on the forearm. (Touch them in the wrong place, and be responsible for your own actions!) It is a touch on the forearm for one to two seconds. As a rule, the forearm is not considered an intimate part of the body, but it is an intimate enough area to make a connection.

▶▶ *Use the Magic Touch on the forearm when you want to make an unconscious, unspoken connection.*
(1 to 2 seconds)

Gueguen concludes that managers should encourage all staff to 'touch more', saying that employees feel more fulfilled, and customers feel more content and satisfied too. Who would have known that a simple touch could make everyone so happy?

I know you were wondering about Gueguen's other persuasion study on hitchhiking. For the record then, here is the account of what happened:

> To test the effect of a woman's bust size on the rate of help offered, 1,200 male and female French motorists were tested in a hitchhiking situation. A 20-year-old female confederate wore a bra that permitted variation in the size of cup to vary her breast size. She stood by the side of a road frequented by hitchhikers and held out her thumb to catch a ride. Increasing the bra size of the female hitchhiker was significantly associated with an increase in number of male drivers, but not female drivers, who stopped to offer a ride.

(Is anyone actually surprised by the result of this research?)

Changing position

For some years now, I've been a very awkward restaurant customer. It's just I really don't like the standard restaurant table layout for two people, where one sits opposite the other. I found whenever I sat at 45 degrees to someone in a restaurant instead of opposite them, we seemed to have a better time. Of course, when you think about it, this makes sense. Facing someone directly is seen as confrontational. Like a kind of squaring up. Sitting at 45 degrees (or even virtually alongside them) is more friendly, conspiratorial.

So why do restaurants keep laying out tables like this? I went to the super-posh eaterie The Ivy in LA recently. My friend and I walked in and there, laid in front of us, were row after row of tables for two with seating directly opposite each other. They were so tightly bunched together I couldn't do my usual trick and get the staff to switch the table around. Grrr. I was physically closer to the strangers sitting to the left and right of me than I was to my friend sitting opposite me.

A more persuasive position is at 45 degrees to the other person, or even virtually next to them. And it's not only about persuasiveness; you may also find it's much easier to form a bond with someone when sitting or standing at this angle.

So yes, I'm the awkward one in restaurants who asks for the tables to be moved around and reset. The change in position results in a more comforting and more relaxed atmosphere. I know it's not always convenient, but when possible, you may well find it results in better rapport and communication. This applies when you're standing and talking to somebody as well as when seated.

▶▶ *In the workplace, in a meeting, with friends or with family, change position to improve communication to get what*

you want. Position yourselves on two corners of a table at a 45-degree angle, rather than directly opposite.
(1 minute)

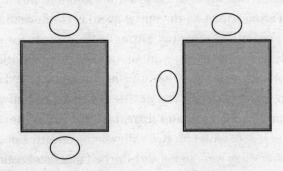

Poor communication position   Good communication position

When you improve your communication, you make the other person more receptive to you, and then you can start to be more persuasive too.

The most persuasive word in the world?

The word *because* has a special power in the English language. It is one of the most used words in hypnosis, and studies have shown that it has a strangely hypnotic effect on us because we often accept what comes after the word *because* without really stopping to consider it. Scary! In the most famous study, social psychologist Ellen Langer and her colleagues found that they could jump to the front of the queue at the photocopier more often simply by using the word *because* and then a statement. They tried three different lines.

'May I use the Xerox machine because I'm in a rush?'
(94 per cent success rate)

'Excuse me, I have five pages. May I use the Xerox machine?' (60 per cent success rate)

'May I use the Xerox machine because I have to make some copies?' (93 per cent success rate)

The final *because* is a very poor reason. But look at the stats. It still had a 93 per cent success rate. We seem to accept the word *because* without even listening to the reason itself, allowing it to become a reason in itself. As Dr Robert Cialdini tells us in his excellent book *Influence: The Psychology of Persuasion*, the word *because* triggers an 'automatic compliance response', which means we simply accept what comes next. As he says, 'It works because it works.'

Master hypnotists and hypnotherapists also understand the power of the word *because*. It is one of their most effective 'trance' words. You can have fun with it too. Trainer and author Jamie Smart encourages people to ask for a discount in a shop, 'because I'd like to have a discount'. He says using such a 'lame reason' is a good idea because it serves as a good reminder of just how powerful the word is. And he reckons it works about 50 per cent of the time.

▶▶ *When you want to get your way, use the word* because *to increase your persuasiveness. People seem to react to* because *as if it were a reason in itself. It works:*

▶▶ *Because the research suggests the average respondent is more likely to accept what you say*

▶▶ *Because people unconsciously accept that a valid reason comes after the word* because

▶▶ *Just because!* (1 second – simply drop into conversation when appropriate)

How could you use this in everyday life? Perhaps something slightly more exciting than getting some photocopies done?

Back to Karen, the gym manager. She'd been struggling to sell private sessions. But fast forward a few weeks and Karen had four new personal training clients. And she swore that the second magic shortcut was the reason.

In the past, if someone had walked over to reception to talk about personal training, Karen had stood behind the reception desk, facing them straight on as she talked to them. Now, whenever someone came over to discuss one-to-one training, she came out from reception and stood next to them as she talked. Sometimes she strolled with the client to the big windows that overlook the gym, and stood next to them looking out as they talked about the benefits of personal training. This resulted in longer chats, and the clients seemed more relaxed and keen to open up.

TO-DO LIST: REMINDERS

▶▶ **Use the Magic Touch on the forearm when you want to make an unconscious, unspoken connection.** (1 to 2 seconds)

▶▶ **Change position. In the workplace, in a meeting, with friends or with family, change position to improve communication to get what you want. Sit at a 45-degree angle, rather than directly opposite. The same applies when you're standing up.** (1 minute max to shift things around)

▶▶ **The most persuasive word. When you want to get your way, use the word** *because* **to increase your persuasiveness. People seem to react to** *because* **as if it were a reason in itself.** (Works in seconds)

CHAPTER 2

Write beautifully persuasive emails

Sophie had recently fallen out with a major client over email. The client had made a mistake and Sophie believed he was paying for advertising at a cheaper rate than he should have been. It was his error, not hers.

Sophie tried to gently let him know this, but the email exchange had escalated and her client had been quite rude. In any other walk of life, Sophie would have simply told him to where to go – he was well out of order. But he was a client.

Even so, she was struggling to control her temper when she read his formal emails detailing all his problems. And as for the language he used: 'implementation of core strategies . . . customer-based initiatives . . . organisation management'; why did some people have to talk like that? And why did her biggest client have to be so hard to get along with?

Our email relationships need to be managed in just the same way as we manage relationships in person. When you can get good rapport on email, you'll find others more receptive and yourself becoming more persuasive. So first we'll look at making a good general connection over email. And then getting a 'yes' for a specific request.

General email connection

▶▶ *How to really read an email*
▶▶ *How to really reply to an email*

Specific requests

▶▶ *Give an order that doesn't seem like an order (very useful)*
▶▶ *Yes Man and Yes Woman*
▶▶ *Ask a question that it is impossible to say no to*

How to *really* read an email

My friend Martin and his girlfriend just couldn't stop arguing. They fought so much and I couldn't understand why. When they'd first got together, they'd seemed such a good couple. Then my friend showed me some emails and texts that they'd sent to each other and things became clearer. '*Look*, it's *clear* that you simply can't *see* what I'm trying to get across here', he would write. 'I just *feel* really bad', she would reply.

We experience the world with our five senses: seeing, hearing, feeling, smelling and tasting. Most of us have one sense that we tend to favour over others. For instance, I'm very visual, so the way something *looks* is really important to me, perhaps more important than the way it *feels*.

And this was the problem with Martin and his girlfriend. He used lots of visual language and she favoured physical, touchy-feely language. The result – communication breakdown.

When you can work out what sense or senses somebody else favours, you can use this to get on with them (and consequently get your way) much more quickly and successfully.

They'll give you all the clues you need in the language they use in their emails. If they use lots of visual words and phrases then their visual sense is strong (*'Looks* good, I *see* what you mean, etc.'). If they use lots of auditory words and phrases then the way stuff sounds is very important to them ('I *hear* what you're *saying, sounds* good, etc.'). And if they use lots of touchy-feely words, then their physical/kinaesthetic sense is highly developed ('It *feels* like the right thing to do, I'm going *cold* on the idea, etc.').

These are the three main senses, so we'll focus on them.

▶▶ *Go over an email you've been sent today. What senses pop up again and again? How does this person experience the world?* (1 minute)

Why is all this important?

Martin was gutted. His relationship with his girlfriend seemed to be falling to pieces. I was already struck by the contrast in the way they related their experience of the world to each other in their emails and texts, and I thought it might be useful to explore how this might hold the key to the challenges in their relationship.

I suggested Martin started focusing on matching his language to hers in emails and in conversation too. And to talk about *his* feelings (not easy for many guys) and to notice when she did the same. Just this heightened awareness meant they stopped arguing so much. He started to get a *grasp* on how she was *feeling* and was *softer* with her when they might have originally had a heated argument. In other words, when she talked about the way she was *feeling*, he now did too. Eventually, they both developed a better understanding of each other's language and, more importantly, how the other experienced the world.

How to really reply to an email

Body language experts talk about subtly 'mirroring' the body language that somebody uses and how this will help to gain 'rapport'. You've probably heard the kind of thing: if they cross their legs you do too, hopefully without making yourself look like a total weirdo in the process. These ideas behind getting rapport don't just apply to body language. They apply to every area of communication, including – of course – language.

▶▶ *Now that you know what to look out for in an email, send it right back. Change your language to be more visual, auditory or physical as appropriate. Make it subtle rapport-building, rather than outright mimicry.* (1 minute to check email before sending)

▶▶ *In addition, reflect the style of email that you've been sent. If someone has signed off 'Best Wishes', then do the same (or 'Yours', 'Thanks', 'Cheers', whatever they use). In a brief email, how can you 'click' better with the other person? (1 minute)*

HINT

■ Here's an email example, and how I might reply.

Dear Tony,

> I had the meeting with your friend Sarah today. I must admit she sounded very knowledgeable when I asked her for her experience. I'm going to listen to recommendations from my colleagues on what to do next. But can I ask you what you think too?

Best,

Jo

Dear Jo,

> That's great that you met Sarah for a chat, and I hear what you're saying about her. I can tell you she's a sound person, and it'd be awesome if you were to hire her, but obviously the final decision is your call.

Best,

Tony

■ Did you spot the auditory language in my reply? *Chat, hear, saying, tell, sound, call.* And then matching the style, spacing and sign-off of her email? People like people who are like them, and you can powerfully build rapport when you reply to an email like this.

■ Sometimes you might find that people use very technical, non-sensory language, like Sophie's client. That's fine. It's sometimes known as the 'Auditory Digital' method of experiencing the world, and again the way to reply is to reflect their style of communicating. In this instance, you too can write about 'implementation of core strategies ... customer-based initiatives ... and organisation management'. It might look or feel silly but it won't be to them because that's how they experience and reflect the world around them. Remember to still look out for the senses, too.

Give an order that doesn't seem like an order

We've already looked in general terms at getting rapport on email. Now let's look at specific requests for compliance.

Softeners

You want somebody to do something, but simply 'ordering' them to do it would seem rude. Simple. Add a softener. These simply work by 'softening' a demand. But the order is still there.

If you were to say to your other half, 'Make me a cup of tea!', they might well say, 'Make it yourself and stop ordering me about!' However, if you were to say, 'Darling, I wonder if you might perhaps make me a cup of tea', they might well make it for you, since you asked them so nicely.

Except the sneaky thing is you still gave them exactly the same order. The same words are in that sentence in the same arrangement, they're just softened. (Of course, some people would still get the same, 'Make it yourself' response, but you are definitely increasing your chances.)

These softeners are especially important in emails, where you can't convey tone. Good softeners to use are:

▶▶ *I wonder*
▶▶ *Maybe*
▶▶ *Might*
▶▶ *Perhaps* *(1 minute max to tag onto the start or end of relevant sentences)*

'I wonder if you might start to practise these now' sounds a bit softer than simply: 'Practise these now.'

Compare these two emails. The order is exactly the same. But in the second, I've used a softener.

> Mark,
> Finish that project by 3 p.m. tomorrow.
> Tony

> Mark,
> I wonder if I could ask you to finish that project by 3 p.m. tomorrow – it'd be much appreciated.
> Tony

I have put exactly the same order in the second email, but it appears more polite and reasonable when softened. However, it is still an order and note there is no question mark.

Yes Man and Yes Woman

This section is inspired by the Jim Carrey film *Yes Man*. Follow the instructions below and you can start to find Yes Men and Yes Women all around you.

Human beings are creatures of habit and once they get into a habit they find it hard to break it. And you can get people into the habit of saying 'yes'. This technique also works because we like to be considered consistent with what we've said previously. So if we say 'yes' a few times, the desire to be consistent plus the force of habit make it more likely we will say 'yes' again. So, get them saying 'yes' now...

1. *Ask a number of questions where the answer is definitely 'yes'. Be subtle. After the third 'yes', you then ask the question where you want the answer to be 'yes'.*
   (1 minute)

2. *You can also do this with statements. Make a number of statements that are known to be true. Then make a statement which you would like someone to accept as true. (1 minute)*

HINT

■ Here's an example.

Dear Sean,

Thanks for coming to our open day last week. It was so sunny, wasn't it? And packed out with people. It was great you stayed until 8 o'clock. Did you have a good time?

Best,
Tony

It was so sunny, wasn't it? (YES)

Packed out with people (YES)

It was great you stayed until 8 (YES – TRUE)

Did you have a good time? (Desired Answer = YES)

■ Alternatively the final question could also be a statement. Like this.

Dear Sean,

Thanks for coming to our open day last week. It was so sunny, wasn't it? And packed out with people. It was great you stayed until 8 o'clock. What a great time we had.

Best,
Tony

Ask a question that it is impossible to say no to

Compare the two sentences:

'Would you like to come to the gig tomorrow night?'

'How much would you like to come to the gig tomorrow night?'

The first question has essentially two possible answers – yes or no. It's very hard to say a simple 'no' to the second question because it just doesn't fit the question. The second question presupposes that, at some level, the person wants to go to the gig, it's just a question of how much. Here are some others.

'How interested are you in buying this product?'

'How much better do you feel?'

'How easy would it be for you to pop over tomorrow afternoon?'

You can also use an 'either/or' question in the same way.

'Would you rather meet tonight at 7 p.m. or 7.30 p.m.?'

When answering a question like that, it's impossible to say 'no'. Sure, you could say, 'I don't want to meet at either time', and sometimes people will. But you eliminate the answer 'no' with an either/or question.

Sophie approached her major client in two separate ways. Firstly, in general terms, she looked at making more of an email connection. As we saw, he used 'Auditory Digital' language and she made an effort to reply in similar terms. She was particularly pleased with a special line she came up with about 'making organisational changes to ensure a more effective ongoing strategy'. She was actually slightly worried it would appear she was taking the mickey. But it worked rather well. His tone softened and he seemed to have fewer objections.

And then, on specific points, she started to give him some either/or questions. The difference was amazing. His replies were transformed. She felt so much more in control of the situation, and he was coming back with a 'yes' much more often. Even in the instances when he clearly wasn't interested in either option, his response was still considerably less blunt than a simple 'no'.

TO-DO LIST: REMINDERS

Really read that email. Check your email for the language that a person uses. What sense pops up again and again? How does this person experience the world? (1 minute)

Mirror your reply. Now that you know what to look out for in terms of language, send it back. Change your language to be more visual, auditory or physical as appropriate. (1 minute)

Use **softeners** to make orders or requests more acceptable. Examples: I wonder, maybe, might, perhaps. (1 minute)

Yes Man and Yes Woman. Ask a number of questions or make a number of statements where the answer is definitely yes. Be subtle. After the third question or statement, you then ask the question where you want the answer to be yes. (1 minute)

Make it impossible to say no. Ask 'either/ or' or presupposition questions to make it impossible for someone to simply say no. 'How interested are you in buying this product?', 'How much better do you feel?', 'Would you rather practise these techniques now or a bit later on?' (1 minute)

CHAPTER 3

Raise more for charity than you ever dreamed possible

Damian was taking part in the Great North Run for the first time and was desperate to raise as much money as possible. He was running it for a cancer charity in memory of his nan so it was a cause very close to his heart.

However, it had been a while since he'd done something to raise money for charity and he wasn't quite sure of the best way to go about it. Should he send out a message on Facebook? Should he email old friends individually? Or should he simply go 'old skool' and walk round the office with a pen and a piece of paper? Damian simply wanted to make sure he raised as much money as possible for the charity.

What could be better than putting your new-found persuasion skills to good use by making lots of money for a deserving cause? Follow these steps in turn and notice how much more money you start to raise.

1. Foot-in-the-door technique

Hmm. Foot-in-the-door sounds bad, doesn't it? For some reason I think of a creepy salesman turning up at my house trying to sell me insurance. But give the foot-in-the-door theory a chance. This technique has helped save lives, raise environmental awareness and make money for charity. And it's going to help you do that too.

The theory is that somebody is more likely to agree to a significant request when they've already agreed to a smaller, related request.

In 1983 a group of researchers found they could increase donations to charity with this technique. Schwarzwald, Bizman and Raz asked a group of people to make a donation to a charity; however, before being asked, some had already been asked to sign a petition simply agreeing with the aims of the charity. The ones who'd signed the petition were more likely to donate.

In 1993 two different researchers, called Taylor and Booth-Butterfield, found that foot-in-the-door could help prevent drink-driving. They discovered drunks were found to be more likely to call for a taxi rather than drive home if they'd previously signed a petition against drink-driving. And foot-in-the-door seems to work whether the commitment is written or verbal. For example, home-owners who'd made a verbal commitment to recycling were then more likely to put a sticker in their windows saying, 'We recycle and we do it right' (Arbuthnot 1976–77).

1. *Ask a small, general question to get an initial verbal commitment from people about giving something to your charity fundraising effort. This can be as simple as 'I'm running the marathon for charity soon, can I put you on my list of potential donors?' (1 minute per donor)*

2. *You have your (metaphorical) foot wedged in the door. Congratulations. Proceed to step 2.*

2. The disproportionate influence of your two most generous friends

What do Bill Gates, Mark Zuckerberg, Warren Buffett and George Lucas have in common? Apart from being seriously rich, they've all signed up to givingpledge.org, a website where super-wealthy Americans pledge to give most of their money away. It's always at least 50 per cent, and in the case of Warren Buffett, he's pledged to give 99 per cent of his entire fortune away. It seems that the greater the number of wealthy individuals who sign up to the pledge, the more follow suit and come forward (40 when launched in August 2010, eighteen more in the five months afterwards). As humans, we're greatly influenced by other people and the community around us. Givingpledge is making the most of that.

The other day I logged onto the justgiving website and made a charity donation to my friend. What was the first thing I did when I went on her page? I took a look down the list at some of the other donations and comments. I then donated myself.

A while later, as I looked at my pledge on the page, I realised I'd donated the same amount as most of the people underneath my name. I realised that I'd unconsciously made a judgement on what to donate based on what others had given. Just like the super-rich on Bill Gates' website, I'd been influenced by the actions of those around me (but sadly donated rather less than Warren Buffett).

How can you exploit this knowledge to raise more money for charity than you'd ever dreamed possible?

1. *Pick your two most generous friends. The ones you know you can count on to give, and give generously.*

2. *Give them a quick call, and explain the disproportionate influence of your two most big-hearted friends when it comes to giving money. Explain that if they make a generous initial donation, not only will you be hugely grateful, but that other people will be more likely to donate more. Perhaps promise also to return the favour when they come to raising money for a cause close to their heart in the future. (1 minute per donor)*

   (NB You can use 'the most persuasive word in the world' from Chapter 1 to help make your case, and some of the softening language and question techniques from Chapter 2, if they help.)

My friend Becca used this technique brilliantly. She rang up her first friend and said, 'Look, I want to get a group of my best mates to each donate £200 for this particular charity night. I know it's a lot, but will you do it?' Her friend said yes. Wow. Very generous. A great start.

Then Becca called another friend and told him the same thing. Being a silly competitive male he decided to donate £201, to simply out-do his friend by a pound. This gave Becca an idea. She would offer a special prize to the person who donated the most. After that, she said, it was easy to get three more friends to donate a pound more every time. She'd raised over £1000 before she'd even started, and what was interesting was that she'd set an example for others to donate more than they normally would.

Once you've gained large donations from your two most generous friends, then the precedent is set and others may be influenced to give more. And you are good to go to Step 3.

3. Make every request individual and special

'Diffusion of responsibility' is what happens when people in groups allow something to happen that would never happen if those people were by themselves. It occurs because individual responsibility is not assigned.

Malcolm Gladwell famously talks about this in his bestselling book *The Tipping Point* when he quotes the tragic example of Kitty Genovese. She was murdered in New York as she walked home. As detectives investigated the killing, they were astonished to discover that thirty-eight of her neighbours saw and heard her die from their apartments, but not one called the police. Gladwell cites this as an example of diffusion of responsibility and says, 'Had she been attacked on a lonely street with just one witness, she might have lived.'

In the world of emails, Facebook messaging and group texts, there are more excuses for diffusion of responsibility than ever. That's why you need to request help from individuals, not groups.

I received a group email one morning from my friend Matt asking me to take part in a sporting event in six months' time. There were forty people on the email. I admit that I forgot about the email and never ended up answering. Days later, I had an individual email from Matt. He asked how I was, and if I wanted to take part in the event? Because he'd addressed me individually, there was now a personal responsibility on me to reply, so of course I did.

Diffusion of responsibility often equals a sad indifference when people are raising money for charity. What a shame. You might be raising money for a worthy, brilliant cause, but you sent a group email to 100 people so there is no individual responsibility to reply.

However, send 100 individual emails and there is a personal responsibility on every single person to at least respond. And then hopefully give as well.

1. *Contact each individual you'd like to donate by email/ facebook message/letter. Personalise the message with their name and perhaps a line or two unrelated to the charity push. Then be explicit and tell them exactly what*

you'd like them to do and how much some people have donated already. You can copy and paste most of this to save time. (1 minute per message)

(NB Make your message as persuasive as possible by using the techniques in Chapter 2, Write beautifully persuasive emails.)

Remember, in the age of digital communication, it's very tempting for us to cut corners by writing one message, and cc'ing it to 10, 100 or 1000 people. If you do this, when you click 'Send', diffusion of responsibility will mean your response rates are lower. Persuade each individual in a minute. Make every request personal and special.

Damian followed the steps. Firstly, he went round his office and told everybody he was running the marathon. His colleagues were excited and congratulated him on doing something so worthwhile. At that point, he put his foot-in-the-door with this line. 'Thanks, dude, can I put you on my list of potential donors?' He had a 100 per cent success rate on that one. Who was going to say no to such a small and innocent request?

Then Damian asked two close friends to make an especially generous donation, and explained how this would help his fundraising effort.

Finally, he made all his charity requests by email. He made them individual and special to the person involved, and – clever this – he reminded them of the smaller commitment they'd previously made.

From: Damian

To: Dan

Subject: **Me hobbling round the Great North Run for charity.**

Hey, Dan, how's it going? Hope the football is still going well.

I know you said I could put you on my list of potential donors for the big charity push I'm making for the Great North Run. That was really kind of you, so here's the information. The big day is almost here, and I'm raising money for Cancer Research. You can see some of the other donations and messages of support by clicking **here**.

Thanks so much, and see you for a kickabout once I've recovered from the run!

Damian

The middle paragraph was copied and pasted, but the email was still individual and special to Dan.

Damian followed up his emails with personal enquiries on the phone or in person, just to give slow responders a bit of extra encouragement. But most didn't need it. Steps 1, 2 and 3 combined perfectly in each individual email. The take-up was huge, and right from the start Damian was surprised at how large many of the donations were. As it turned out, a number of those who donated even followed the precedent of his two original friends and matched their generosity.

Damian raised more money than he ever dreamed possible. And he was proud to do that in memory of his nan.

TO-DO LIST: REMINDERS

Get your *'foot-in-the-door'*. Get an initial very small verbal commitment from each donor. This can be as simple as 'I'm running the marathon for charity soon, can I put you on my list of potential donors?' (1 minute per donor)

Set the bar high. Pick two extremely generous friends and ask them to donate lots. This will then have an impact on the amount others give as people tend to be influenced by the actions of those around them. (1 minute per donor)

Make every request personal. Contact each potential donor individually. Personalise the message to avoid diffusion of responsibility. If appropriate, subtly remind them of their earlier small verbal commitment. (1 minute per message)

CHAPTER 4

How to make the most of Facebook

Ruth couldn't work it out. She'd sent a Facebook invite for her birthday party to all her closest friends over three days ago. It was going to be fancy dress – what could be more fun? But hardly anyone was accepting. In fact, the only comments that people were leaving on the event wall were from people who couldn't come. 'Sorry, Ruthie, I'd love to but I'm in Paris that weekend, have a good one x.' 'Ooooh, that sounds so fun, but Dave's down for the weekend. Have a fun and happy b'day!!'

Only seven of her normally reliable friends had accepted and she had invited 105 people. She also had 11 'maybes', which she felt was normally a polite way of being blown out.

It was now Monday, and the party was five days away. Ruth had that horrible feeling the week before a party when you're just not sure whether it's going to be a success. Because, as she herself admitted, it was all starting to look like a 'Facebook fail'.

So you have an important status update or post that you want lots of people to see? Perhaps you're selling your car? Organising a club night? Or you've lost your phone and need everyone's number? Or – like Ruth – perhaps your party is turning out to be a bit of a damp squib?

Time to get on Facebook and start using the system to get yourself noticed and make yourself more persuasive. In this chapter you'll discover:

▶▶ *How to use 'social proof' to enhance your Facebook experience*
▶▶ *The right questions to ask to get your posts top of the news feed*
▶▶ *How singles can make themselves 'more attractive' on Facebook*
▶▶ *How to create a buzz around your party on Facebook*

Let's start by looking to understand how Facebook works, and start to use it to your and your friends' advantage.

Recently it was my friend Rich's birthday. As he watched the birthday messages on his wall come in throughout the day, he posted a short status update.

Rich Sweetman
Well, am genuinely chuffed, and somewhat humbled by all the birthday messages you guys sent me! I have had a great day, so thanks to each and every one of you ... However, although 82 wall posts comments is VERY strong, wouldn't it be great to get to 100!!?! Ha ha ... Crack on ...

To his friends, it was typical Rich – funny, silly and infectious. Before long, people were wishing him happy birthday in reply to this status. And posting funny messages about how desperate he was to want lots of messages.

As he crept up through the nineties mid-afternoon, and this particular post remained resolutely at the top of my news feed, I noticed that every single reply had been 'liked' by at least one person. I checked who it was, and … it was Rich himself. I left another reply. 'Ha, you are too desperate … liking stuff on your own wall.' He sent me a message. 'It all helps, mate!' And then 'liked' his own post yet again.

Rich understands how Facebook works though. He passed 100 with ease, and he was using 'social proof' all the way.

How to get your posts ranked top of everybody else's news feed

Social proof is the concept that if lots of other people are doing something, then it must be worthwhile for us to do so too. Put simply, it means we often look to others to guide our own actions. It's not necessarily right, but we will often act on it anyway.

A few examples: a Facebook group with hundreds of thousands of followers gains social proof from having those followers. If one of your Facebook posts gets fifty-one 'likes' on it, again that provides validation of the post to others. And you've probably also noticed the feeling you get when lots of people comment positively on a photo of yours. That's because you're revelling in the warm glow you're receiving from powerful social proof.

Facebook itself appears to use this social proof to determine what we read in our 'news feed'. An investigation by *Daily Beast* journalist Thomas E. Weber found 'to get exposure on Facebook, you need friends to interact with your updates'. If you find Facebook more addictive than crack, this will make total sense to you, as you'll have already noticed how more commented on posts or stories tend to jump to the top of your news feed. The theory appears to often be that the more feedback a post receives, the more of interest it is to everyone else (There's that social proof again.)

There also seem to be other factors at play, such as whether a person looks at 'Top News' or 'Most Recent', and how much you interact with another person in the first place – but using social proof can be a powerful way to get your message to more people.

So, when you want to rank highly in the news feed:

1. *Finish your post with a question, rather than a statement. Engage people into a response. It doesn't actually matter what the response is, as long as people do respond. (1 minute)*

2. *Send an individual private message to a few close friends. Do it straightaway. Tell them that this status update is important, so could they comment on it and/ or 'like' it. By the way, you might think this a bit uncool, but this is the way to build unstoppable social proof momentum. What's the alternative? Don't do it, and no one will read your important post. (1 minute)*

3. *Reply to any questions/answers that people post on the status. This both engages in conversation and boosts the amount of feedback.* (A few seconds)

4. *Put a link to another web page in your status. This, says Thomas E. Weber, trumps a simple status update as it 'drives user engagement with Facebook'.* (1 minute)

5. *My mate Rich would say 'like' every reply too. It will help – true. But some might say that is a Facebook fail! So – your call.* (A few seconds)

Then watch as the social proof takes effect. The more people that comment, the more others will see that this post is socially accepted and be more likely to get involved. In addition, previous posters get updates on other comments, keeping them engaged. Some social media experts say if you want to take an even more direct route, you could write directly on each of your 674 friends' walls. But I would find this highly annoying. You're better off following the above steps.

In an entirely unscientific but fun study on my Facebook public page wall (facebook.com/tonywrighton), I put this all to the test. Facebook provides data on public page 'impressions' (i.e., amount of time a post appears in a news feed). I recently posted a short, fun, open question about Facebook and persuasion skills. I then contacted some friends to explain the experiment and made sure within an hour there were a number of responses and some 'likes'.

After 48 hours I compared the number of page impressions to five recent posts that had received far less feedback.

When compared to these 'less popular' posts, the study post consistently received at least 90 per cent more impressions, in some cases (i.e. the least 'popular' posts) rising to 300 per cent.

Social proof on Facebook can create unstoppable momentum, and big brands are taking advantage. Some of the world's top marketers are devoting huge resources to Facebook – and who can blame them when you read these extraordinary stats from Facebook's director Emily White. She recently revealed that Coca-Cola's official site receives approximately 270,000 monthly unique users, but 22.5 million on Facebook. Almost 100 times more people visit Coca-Cola's Facebook page than visit the official site.

What's the relevance of Coca-Cola to the above exercise on getting your posts ranked higher? Well, let me come back to perhaps the most important thing – to engage your followers by asking an 'open question'. Maybe one of the reasons that Coca-Cola's page is so popular is that it engages its followers so effectively. I just checked their most recent post at the time of writing.

Coca-Cola: What's your best memory of drinking a Coke? 18th January at 03.21.

12,884 people like this.
View all 7,840 comments

Very simple open question. Over 20,000 responses. Nice.

Not to be outdone, Pepsi has a whole section called 'Have

A Great Idea?' At the time of writing, they are accepting '1000 ideas every month' from Pepsi fans. Judging from the crazy level of feedback on the Pepsi Facebook page, people are loving getting engaged in this way.

Remember, when you ask an open question that engages your followers, you're more likely to get a high level of response.

How singles can make themselves 'more attractive' on Facebook

Ever heard of 'mate choice copying'? If the research is anything to go by, it's happening on Facebook right now.

Researchers at Duke University and the University of California found that when we're alongside someone attractive in a photo, people find *us* more attractive too! And when we're alongside somebody not so blessed in the looks department, our perceived attractiveness goes down too.

They took a large group of men and women, all of whom described themselves as 'straight', and showed them pictures of a 'potential mate'. In some pictures, the potential mate was standing alongside someone the participants were told was an ex, who they were now no longer with.

The researchers consistently found that potential mates were thought to be more attractive when they were alongside somebody else 'attractive' than when they were alone. In addition, the potential mates were found to be less attractive when they were alongside a partner perceived to be unattractive.

Interestingly, the researchers also tracked eye movement, and every single participant spent time looking at the partner in the photo, despite only being asked to assess the potential mate.

This is mate choice copying.

What does this tell us about Facebook? According to this theory, it tells us that when we post photos, our attractiveness is partly about *who we are alongside*, as well as the way we look ourselves. It'll make you look at your Facebook profile in a whole different way – trust me.

Moral of the story: if you're single, get loads of photos of yourself alongside hotties. This action alone is probably not going to help you pull Brad Pitt but, according to the above research, it may well enhance your prospects.

How to create a buzz around your party on Facebook

When you organise a group event on Facebook, sending out a group invite can encourage the same lack of individual response that we looked at in Chapter 3, Raise more money for charity than you ever dreamed possible, and can do your cool event some serious damage. To start creating that massive buzz, you can use all the techniques above to get visible and create excitement. After you've done that, it's time to get personal…

1.   *Set up an event page on Facebook for your party. Don't invite anyone just yet.* (1 minute)

2. *Contact your ten closest friends with personal private messages. Ask them if they can come to your party.* (Less than 1 minute per message)

3. *If they reply 'yes' – send them an invite to the event page. Then reply to their message, ask if they'll accept the invite, and write a message on the wall related to the party. (What they'll be bringing, what they'll wear, etc.) If they reply 'maybe', reply asking them to accept the invite you send them. If they reply 'no', reply back but don't invite them to the event.* (Less than 1 minute per message)

4. *Once some buzz is building, invite another batch of friends in exactly the same way. Do not send a collective invite without an individual message first, as you want to avoid that 'diffusion of responsibility'.*

5. *Watch as you create excitement around your event. Instead of waiting and hoping for people to respond, your wall fills with positive party messages, and others who are invited to see the page realise that this is going to be an occasion to remember and spontaneously respond to the social proof that has built up.*

6. *If anyone does leave a message on your wall saying they can't make it, private message them back saying how disappointed you are. And then consider deleting their post. Up to you, of course, but do you really want them killing your party buzz? You want people wondering if they're going to be on the hottest guestlist of the year, not leaving sad boo-hoo messages about how they can't come.* (1 minute)

Of course all this is the opposite of what Ruth did with her party. The only 'buzz' around her birthday event on Facebook was a couple of sad wall posts from people who couldn't come.

I happened to be at her house on that Monday night when she showed me her wall. I felt guilty. I'd been invited to her birthday party but, like everyone else, I hadn't got round to replying because there was no individual responsibility on me to do so.

We set about rescuing the situation and the party. Firstly, the five of us in her front room that evening accepted her invite and posted on her event wall details of what we were going to dress up as. Then we got Ruth to delete all the 'sorry can't make it' messages on the same wall. Finally, she sent a brief message to ten of her closest friends, asking if they were going to come. When eight replied 'yes' within a day, she asked if they'd reply to the event invite and post something good on the wall. Finally, she was starting to create that buzz. And sure enough, others started getting involved too.

FINAL BIT ON FACEBOOK: Facebook alters and changes its algorithms all the time, not just because it's one of the fastest growing and most successful companies in the world but also to keep the likes of us guessing and, of course, to further its own success. So whilst the above is all helpful in making yourself more visible and persuasive on Facebook, it's useful to remember this and connect with people in 'real life' as much as possible too.

TO-DO LIST: REMINDERS

Get seen more on Facebook. **To get as many impressions as possible for your post, finish it with a question, ask some friends to comment and reply to any questions/answers that people post on it. This both engages friends in the conversation and boosts the amount of feedback, making your post more visible.** (One minute per post)

Make yourself more attractive. **Take advantage of 'mate choice copying' if you're single by making sure you are alongside attractive people in photos on your page. According to research, potential mates will see these photos and assess you as more desirable.**
(One minute to post new photos)

Create a buzz **around your party by sending private invites before sending any group invite.**
(One minute per invite)

The importance of buzz. **Manage the buzz on your event wall by encouraging excited comments and getting rid of those 'I can't come' messages. As the buzz develops, these messages will look after themselves.**

CHAPTER 5

Get that pay rise

Jayne had been working in the same job for five years. Each April she was given an assessment for the previous twelve months. If she achieved a mark of 3 or above out of 5 on this, then the company would guarantee a pay rise.

For five years in a row, Jayne had scored either 4 or 4.5 on her assessment. And for the past five years, Jayne had received a pay rise of 2 per cent. Which, as she was fond of saying, wasn't even enough to buy her an extra pair of her favourite shoes (Jayne has expensive taste in shoes).

Jayne was particularly annoyed because she knew that friends doing similar jobs in other companies were paid a lot more. But she didn't really want to leave. She was quite comfortable in her work and grateful to have it. So how on earth did she get a proper pay rise?

I thought the title of this chapter might get your attention. As well as using the following techniques in my life, I've spoken to top business leaders, entrepreneurs and negotiators on the subject of getting a pay rise. And as it happens, their message almost always comes down to exactly the same thing.

In order to get what you want, you have to give people what they want. You have to be the best and offer them something that nobody else can. And then… you have to make sure that they realise the value of what you give them, and what would happen if it was taken away.

'Dammit!' you're possibly thinking, 'I've been coasting along in a job I hate for the last three years, not putting any effort in and barely bothering to snarl a "Good morning" to my boss, and despite all that, I was hoping, really hoping, that I could double my salary in one minute.' Hang on there. Don't turn to Chapter 6 just yet. I do still have something for you. Take a look at how this chapter is divided up. How to get a pay rise with:

▸▸ *Value*
▸▸ *Belief*
▸▸ *Relationship*
▸▸ *High-risk one-minute strategies*

If you are the original work dosser who's not adding any value, you're a bit of a chancer and you don't have a relationship with your superiors, it might already be obvious which section of this chapter is for you. Take a deep breath and turn straight to *High-risk one-minute strategies*.

Otherwise, my friend, if you really deserve that pay rise, read on.

Value

I sat opposite one of the UK's leading sports agents in a private members' club in East London. He has clients in the football world as well as TV and showbiz and is used to striking some pretty spectacular deals. The perfect man to help me (and us) make more money. So I cut to the chase. 'All I want to know,' I said, 'is how I do it? What's the secret to going in and tripling someone's wages in one meeting? Next time I have to negotiate, what do I need to do to earn pots more money?'

He took a swig of his whisky and looked up.

'It's all about value. How much value do you have?'

What? I have to admit, I was slightly disappointed. Not some verbal trick to get my boss to double my wages? Or a killer body language move that instantly puts a nought on the end?

But he went on, 'If you're Wayne Rooney, you offer something that very few people around the world can offer, and that is the commodity of goals. You're one of the best strikers in the world, providing a unique level of skill. Then off the pitch, you also offer a unique commodity which is your brand, and that sells millions of shirts and boosts the brand of Manchester United around the world. All this adds up to massive value – on and off the pitch.'

Of course, he had a point, and those top business leaders, entrepreneurs and negotiators all say the same thing. You *must* create as much value as possible for your company. You do this by being the best and providing something unique which nobody else can do. Then you must make sure those who run the company know about it, so you make sure you get the credit you deserve and they feel like they absolutely cannot do without you.

It's not about asking your boss for praise every time you send an email, but simply making sure you get the recognition you deserve for your hard work and dedication.

Pursuing this goal of offering value and dedication to a company will always leave you in a stronger position to negotiate, but of course the title of this book is not *Persuasion Over the Course of a Career* but *Persuade in a Minute*, so let's move on to the nitty-gritty of negotiation itself. Here's how to negotiate around value.

1. *Demonstrate your value to them* (1 minute)

Have a list ready. It is not about why you deserve more money (in fact, money doesn't even get mentioned here), but a list of what you already offer your employers that is unique and that they can't do without. Tell them about all your wins. Show them your value, and your pride in that value.

2. *Create more value for them* (1 minute)

Have a second list ready of how you can add even more value. This could be in many different areas; working longer, pursuing a profitable new business sideline, offering to do the weekend shifts that nobody else wants to do, increasing sales in a particularly difficult area, or offering to get in at 7 a.m. to attend the morning meeting so your boss doesn't have to. Now you're adding real value for them so they can see how important it is that you stay and are well rewarded for it.

3. Create more value for yourself *(1 minute)*

Look, wage negotiations are egotistical minefields. Most of the employers I've worked for have had large egos and a high opinion of themselves. They don't like to be proved wrong, don't like to admit they're wrong and that sense of certainty is probably one of the reasons they've got to the position they're in.

That means that in a wage negotiation, everyone has to feel like they've 'won'. They have to feel like they've emerged victorious and that they haven't lost face. Your job is to create more value for yourself in the deal whilst subtly massaging their ego.

Think of other ways you can add value to your deal. Can you negotiate a performance-related incentive that you previously didn't have? Could you ask for an extra two weeks' holiday a year? (Two extra weeks off is equivalent to a more than 4 per cent pay rise *and* you increase your quality of life.) Or two weeks off at Christmas and New Year – no questions asked? (This is often easier for an employer to agree to since many already have a number of days off over this period.) Or you get no raise this year, but you receive a guaranteed raise of 10 per cent in twelve months' time? (An employer may be more open to this suggestion because the raise is so far in the future.) All of a sudden you're not pushing so hard financially and so some of the emotions and egos are removed. Agreement can be more straightforward and it's easier for them to say the magic word – yes.

The sports agent was big on this third point. As he said to me, 'If you want six and they won't budge from five, take it. Don't be stubborn for the sake of it. Be realistic, accept the salary and look at negotiating on other points. It's always easier once you move away from the pure financials.'

When he said 'six', I had a funny feeling he was talking about six million. So I decided to take his word for it.

Belief

The more sure you are, the more sure you appear. You have to believe in what you're saying, and this is particularly important in negotiation.

This is the first time I've mentioned congruence in this book, but in truth it is a vital part of persuasion. Put simply, most of us are pretty good at sniffing out someone who doesn't believe in what they're saying. Their body language doesn't match their words, their tonality screams 'unsure', and they aren't convincing.

Add to this the probability that the person one is negotiating with has probably done it many times before; they've seen it all and know what to look for.

So be sure that the reasons you've included on those lists we looked at in the previous section are a) what you truly believe, and b) what you can deliver. Otherwise, they'll sniff you out.

Be congruent.

Relationship

It's all about rapport. And not just when you want a raise but in every work and indeed human interaction. Who are you negotiating with? What's the rapport like?

Talk to your boss about their life and things that interest them. Establish a good relationship with them. Make sure you mean it – sincerity is key. See the best in him or her. (Goodness knows this can be challenging – it was particularly difficult with some of the bosses I've had. But you have to do it.)

▶▶ Approach any meeting with respect, courteousness and a smile. Take a minute at the start of the meeting to establish some rapport. *(1 minute on arrival – then chat for as long as they want to on unrelated topics. If they are your senior, let them move the topic on.)*

HINT

■ Ask good, relevant questions.

'What a great win for your team last night!'

'How did your daughter get on in her school play?'

■ Ask good questions, make sure you are actually interested in the answers you get and start to establish permanent rapport. Remember the previous section: if you're only asking to get what you want, they'll sniff you out. Make sure you actually care about the answers.

One more thing. If your boss is extremely businesslike and appears disinterested in gaining rapport, don't give up. Match their businesslike demeanour because this is clearly important to them, but still attempt to relate and engage with them. In this instance you will often be marking yourself out as different from your co-workers, as many of them will pick up on that disinterest and not even make an effort.

High-risk one-minute strategies

TONY'S WARNING: The following persuasion techniques might make you rich. But they might also get you sacked. If you get rich, then it's all because of me. If you get sacked, it's definitely not my fault.

The BIG SALARY BOOM (or it's all about perspective)

Sixteen-year-old Adam earns £10 every time he cleans the next-door neighbour's car. The neighbour always says how pleased he is with Adam's work and now Adam wants to earn £15 per wash. So he asks the next-door neighbour if he could perhaps earn £15 from next time? The neighbour takes a moment to consider this and then expresses the view that yes, Adam does clean his car very well. Would it be possible to compromise – how about £12.50 from now on?

With this technique, you must establish your true figure as the compromise position, not your ideal figure.

Sports and TV agents often negotiate like this: $5 million for a basketball player seems positively cheap when they were originally asking for $18 million. The agent asks for far more than he actually expects because it gives him room to negotiate, and the compromise position is what they wanted all along.

▶▶ *Hit them with the Big Salary Boom. Ask for substantially more than your target figure. Use your judgement of your own personal situation to pick a figure that is as high as possible – almost outrageously so. (1 minute)*

▶▶ *Then proceed to compromise down to your real target.*

If Adam had asked for £25 the next time, what would the neighbour's reaction have been? Possibly, 'Blimey, that's a bit steep. But you do a good job, how about we compromise and say £15 from now on?'

But of course it may also have been, 'Sod off.' So it's a

high-risk strategy. Remember – everyone wants to feel like they've won, and that comes through compromise, so start as high as you can get away with.

Options

Research suggests people are more motivated by the thought of losing something than by the thought of gaining something. If somebody values your work, then the theory is they're going to sweat more at the prospect of losing you.

So tell them you have options.

Herb Cohen, author of *New York Times* bestseller *You Can Negotiate Anything*, is regarded as one of the world's foremost authorities on negotiation. He says:

> If you have a viable option or other alternatives, you can maintain your cool and confidence. And people always have confidence in confident people.

And how does he define the level at which you should approach the meeting? Well this guy has negotiated with NFL players and Soviet Union Arms Control negotiators. He clearly knows his stuff, and here's his verdict.

> You should care, really care ... but not t-h-a-t much.

So with your new attitude of caring, but not t-h-a-t much, here's what you do.

▶▶ *Bring up the question of value and what you are worth, as per earlier in the chapter. However, this time do it differently.*

> *The trick is to subtly let it be known that you are aware of your 'value' in the marketplace, without outright saying that you have other options. Talk about what you are worth rather than what they can afford to pay.* *(1 minute)*

▶▶ *If you do have other options that you are happy to exploit, you can be more explicit. Push hard enough and you'll call their bluff. (Once you've gone too far down this road, it's hard to turn back, and you have to remember the egos involved in negotiation. They have to leave the negotiation happy.)*

▶▶ *Remember: people seem to be more motivated by the thought of losing something.*

Of course this high-stakes game helps if you actually do have options. They will give you that Herb Cohen 'cool and confidence'. If you don't have other offers, then you truly must have balls of steel, because there's always the risk they will tell you to go ahead and leave.

Back to the whisky-swigging sports agent in London. He started a football story about one of the world's top players. 'What happened when Manchester City came in with a monster offer to double Wayne Rooney's money to £200,000 a week?' he asked me. 'His agent was in the perfect situation. His client offers massive *value*, and he had a very public, very lucrative *option* to help him negotiate with confidence. And so Rooney's current club Manchester United matched it, gave him a gigantic deal, and made Wayne Rooney their highest-paid player ever. Easy.'

Let's return to Jayne, who had been working in the same job for five years and, each April, despite a brilliant yearly assessment, received a rubbish pay rise. She started her meeting with her boss by talking about something surprising. Shoes. What do you know, they both loved fancy shoes and spent a good few minutes discussing the merits of one brand over another. They clearly had a good relationship, which was important.

When they eventually moved on to the serious stuff, Jayne's boss congratulated her on once again getting a great assessment and for her hard work over the year. But despite a discussion over the great value Jayne was offering the company, it appeared she was not being offered a decent increase.

So Jayne told her boss about her other options. Despite not really wanting to leave, she'd scoped out some similar companies and one had actually offered her a job on improved terms. The more she'd thought about it, the more she'd come round to the idea, and thought it might be quite fun to work somewhere else for a change.

'In that case,' Jayne's boss said, she would consider 'matching the terms the other company is offering' to keep her.

Jayne was interested, but by now she was negotiating with cool and confidence. So she pushed on to create more value for herself. She said she was grateful for the increased offer but she had been hoping for more. However, she would be prepared to accept the offer if she could have a guaranteed twelve days off over Christmas and New Year each year so she could go and stay with her family in America.

Her boss thought about it, smiled and nodded. Jayne had demonstrated value, negotiated herself more money and created additional value for herself in the deal.

TO-DO LIST: REMINDERS

Value. Demonstrate your existing value to them (1 minute), create more value for them (1 minute), and then create value for yourself in the negotiation. (1 minute)

Belief. Make sure you really believe in yourself, and that you can deliver. Otherwise they'll sniff you out.

Relationship. Always take some time to establish rapport. Take a genuine interest. (1 minute on arrival – then chat for as long as they like. Let them move the topic on)

The high-stakes route 1. Hit them with the Big Salary Boom. Ask for a lot more than your target figure. This sets the bar high and opens room for negotiation and compromise towards your real target. (1 minute)

The high-stakes route 2. Tell them you have other options. Remember, 'People are more motivated by the thought of losing something than gaining something of equal value.' (1 minute)

CHAPTER 6

How to get a seven-year-old to tidy their room

Annette is mum to a little girl called Tilly and also a full-time policewoman. This means mornings are particularly busy as she gets herself ready for work and Tilly ready for school. Every day, before they were about to leave the house for school, Tilly would procrastinate over getting dressed. She just couldn't decide on what she wanted to wear. Annette would be ready to leave and Tilly would still be wearing her pyjamas with all her clothes strewn across the floor. It started to make them late for school and Annette late for work too. And of course Tilly's room would be a mess. Mornings were becoming more and more difficult.

The thing is, Tilly had previously been such a good little girl and – Annette could swear – even better

behaved than many of her friends' children (although of course Annette knew she was just a tiny bit biased). Despite this, she was now playing up in the mornings and Annette wasn't sure how to persuade her to get ready on time and keep her room tidy.

Kids can often be more perceptive than us adults. If we don't give them a good reason, or we're inconsistent, or they spot a flaw in our argument, or they reckon they can get away with something, they'll do it. And, as you'll read in the following examples, that 'something' might be anything that long-suffering Mum and Dad don't want them to do. So hopefully these ideas will give you a fresh perspective on what makes your little angel tick.

All the parents involved in writing this chapter made the point that different things work for different kids and there is no universal rule that works for every child. But the techniques in the list below consistently ranked as the most effective ways of getting your child to tidy his/her room (and other things you want to persuade them to do). Yes, each one takes less than a minute. *And* all these techniques can be relevant in adult persuasion too.

▶▶ *Consistency*
▶▶ *Threat*
▶▶ *Enthusiasm*
▶▶ *Reward v Punishment*
▶▶ *Guilt*
▶▶ *Bribery*
▶▶ *The ultimate room-tidying persuasion tactic*

Consistency

Consistency and commitment are important to us adults. We admire those who are decisive and sure. How confusing and irritating is it when we encounter someone in life who says one thing one day and then something totally different the next?

It's the same, of course, for kids. Sarah is mum to three kids, aged nine, seven and one.

Consistency for me comes in two different areas. The first is that we keep some consistent rules. In the early days, we'd break the rules because we cared so much about making our kids happy. 'Of course they can stay up another half-hour and watch TV with us. What harm can it do?' But then the next time they wanted to stay up and watch and we said no, they'd get upset. 'You let me stay up last time? Why can't I stay up this time?' We hadn't been consistent and they struggled to understand. Now we are consistent with our rules, every time. It was hard at first because we didn't want to play the bad guy. But they know exactly what to expect now, and we are all happier.

The second is routine. Because we have a set routine that never changes, days are less hectic and there are fewer arguments. The kids know what is expected of them at certain points during the day and this is consistent from day to day.

Aurelie is mum to Callum and Iris, and agrees that consistency is crucial, but says sometimes it's good to mix things up.

Routine is so important. We often forget that they are brand new people, constantly learning about this big wonderful world, and in order to learn and remember things, they need to feel safe, happy and relaxed. However, I believe it is also REALLY important to take them out of that strict routine once in a while (starting with a friend's house or a restaurant, and then working up to holidays and unusual destinations). The right balance of routine and new adventures will make them more curious and sociable, and more flexible at home too.

You can use this theory in your life with other adults too. Act consistently in a relationship, or at work, or in any social interaction, and others will learn what to expect from you and how to act to get certain responses. In this way, you can gain increased compliance.

Threat

Threat. Sounds serious, doesn't it. Becky is mum to two gorgeous kids and she says, when used selectively, a threat works very effectively.

When I'm trying to persuade Molly to tidy her room, I think the best way is to threaten the loss of something, for example, no *Spongebob Squarepants* on TV. Another little threat has now spiraled into its own phrase of 'half-book Mum'. Basically, at bedtime, I will only read half a book if she hasn't done what I asked.

On the issue of kids tidying, any *children* reading this could borrow little Bailey's line. Lena lives in Nottingham and Bailey is her seven-year-old son.

Bailey has always been a very good boy. The only time tidying up is ever an issue is when Bailey has a friend over. Afterwards, if it's messy, we ask him to tidy up. If he says no, we have tried telling him he won't be allowed to have friends over again if he won't tidy afterwards. At which point he will reply that 'we have to help too'. To get it done properly we always seem to end up helping! That boy is better at persuasion skills than we are.

Enthusiasm

Samantha is a pre-school teacher and mum of two. She makes chores fun.

Trying to make them do something is much easier if they actually want to do it. I turn it into a game. For example, if it's time to tidy up at the end of the day, I will say, 'Who can put the toys in the basket the fastest?' or 'You put the blue toys in, you put the red toys in.' By making it fun, everyone is happy.

Rachel is mother to six-year-old Luke. She takes it a step further and turns tidying into a song.

I start singing the 'Tidying-up-time song'. It's so silly and catchy, and I turn it into such a game that Luke can't resist joining in. I sound completely ridiculous when singing it, but who cares?

Reward v Punishment

This is perhaps the oldest and most basic persuasion technique in the book. When your child misbehaves at school, they are punished. When they do well, they are (hopefully) rewarded. Do you do the same at home? Without wishing to state the obvious, the theory is this:

Rewards increase the behaviour.
Punishment decreases the behaviour.

But how to reward and how to punish? Mum Samantha makes the point that often the most effective form of reward can be gentle affection and attention.

> You need to be careful about what the reward is. I don't use a sweet or chocolate because then the children get used to it. It's important kids learn to do something simply for the satisfaction of having done it. They get a reward in the form of praise (for example, by me saying, 'Ooh, thanks for helping, look how beautifully tidy the room looks now.').

In Chapter 5, Get that pay rise, we mentioned the theory that shows people are more motivated by the thought of losing something than by the thought of gaining something. Mum of two Becky says this is also true with kids, and this forms the most effective type of punishment.

I really remember wholeheartedly thinking that positivity was the only way to good behaviour, when in actual fact, taking their chocolate buttons away can have much more impact because it's immediate.

Guilt

The emotion of guilt is very persuasive. Sally is a children's nurse and mother of two. She says this about her son Toby:

When Toby was being naughty at school, and nothing was making him behave, I worked the guilt card: 'Mummy is very disappointed in you, Toby.' It works very well.

Do you want your child to feel guilty though? As ever with parenting, it's your call, and if it encourages them to reflect on their actions then it may be useful. However, guilt doesn't work forever, as Samantha says:

Eventually the child will stop feeling guilty and just do what they want to do anyway.

Bribery

Cor, this chapter reads like a list of underhand tactics. All mums and dads know this one though. You promise them something else if they do what you want them to do. It's not subtle, but bribery often works.

We know all about the power of the bribe from adult life; for example, the bartender who receives a big tip early in the evening tends to pour bigger measures. And as mum of three Nikki says, it works the same with kids.

> My middle one hates eating greens. But she'll force them down if there's a bowl of ice-cream on offer afterwards.

The ultimate room-tidying persuasion tactic

This one really made me chuckle. Jane has two daughters, aged ten and eight. She says that most of the above persuasion tactics simply aren't effective. She's tried everything, but thankfully now there is something that seems to work.

> If one of them hasn't tidied their room, or refuses to do it, I have a simple tactic that gets almost miraculous results. I just tell them that if they don't tidy their room, I will pay the other sister their allowance to do it for them. The double whammy threat of losing their allowance and having their sibling mess up all their stuff works every time.
>
> Take it from me: threatening to pay one child another's allowance is an extraordinarily convincing way to get what you want.

Annette's nightmare scenario started to occur every morning. Just as she and daughter Tilly were supposed to be leaving the house for school, Tilly still wouldn't be dressed, resulting in them leaving the house far too late, with Tilly's room strewn with her clothes.

Two things worked. Threat and reward.

'First, I'd say this:

Okay, I'll tell you what. I'm not going to ask you to get dressed again, but when it's time to leave, we're going in whatever you are wearing.' This would inevitably be Tilly's pyjamas, as she hadn't got dressed. Because Tilly didn't want to be embarrassed, she got herself dressed. (Incidentally, I had secretly packed a spare school uniform in the car, in case she had to follow through with the threat.)

A second effective line was:

'If we are late, I will tell your teacher why we are late.'

Annette did not actually have to follow through with either of these threats as she was placing the responsibility to conform on her daughter.

And the thing that worked best was simply rewarding Tilly when she had picked out an outfit and got dressed, and kept her room tidy.

'Gosh, what a beautiful outfit! Well done, Tilly, you look lovely, and you've done very well getting dressed so quickly. And doesn't your room look lovely and tidy.'

Not all techniques work for all children, so work out what works for you from the list below.

Consistency. Keep a consistent set of rules and routines.

Threat. Use threats selectively.

Enthusiasm. Act enthusiastically, by turning room-tidying (or another activity) into a game.

Reward good behaviour.

Guilt. Let your child see how disappointed you are. If they feel guilty about their bad behaviour they may change it next time.

Bribery. 'If you eat your greens, you can have an ice-cream.'

The ultimate room-tidying persuasion tactic. Use to your advantage on siblings!

CHAPTER 7

The sweet, sweet sound that makes friends and wins arguments

David considered himself quite an outgoing and charismatic guy but, he had to admit, when he put himself up against his boss Ralph, Ralph won hands down.

At parties, Ralph had an uncommon knack of remembering each individual person's name. He could remember partners' names as well as children's names. Sometimes it even seemed like he could remember what the pet dog was called. David would watch in admiration as vague acquaintances would flush with pleasure as Ralph remembered that their daughter Molly enjoyed ballet or their son Harvey had a gift for writing.

By comparison, David struggled to remember names.

At the last work party he'd been to, he'd had to whisper to his girlfriend that she would have to introduce herself to people, as he couldn't remember what they were called. The other guests didn't look too impressed and, come to think of it, nor did his girlfriend.

At meetings, Ralph would command the attention of everyone in the room, yet make each individual feel special, whether they were senior managers or office juniors. Those personal skills had a huge effect on customers, who always seemed to enjoy spending time with Ralph. And on the odd occasion Ralph found himself in a work dispute with David, Ralph seemed to be able to firmly disarm and flatter him so effectively that in the end David would end up agreeing with Ralph.

David wanted some of that, too.

The last few chapters have dealt with very specific scenarios for getting what you want. Now let's look at making your whole personality more compelling. Being persuasive is about making people more receptive to your message, and one way you can do that is by using that sweet, sweet sound that people love – the sound of their own name.

The title of this chapter is inspired by Dale Carnegie, who wrote about names in his classic book *How To Win Friends and Influence People*, published in 1936.

Remember that a person's name is to that person the sweetest and most important sound in any language.

The first part of this chapter concentrates on how to remember a name, so you won't be umming and erring and making a terrible first impression, like David at the party. The second looks at how to *use* a name to make yourself more persuasive, like David's boss Ralph.

'Let me introduce you. Whatshisname, meet Thingumybob.'

Most of us are rubbish at remembering names. More often than not, when we're introduced to somebody, we're thinking about making a good impression, keeping the conversation going, being polite, just about anything other than remembering what the hell they're called.

Even worse, there's that awful feeling when you know you have to introduce person A to person B and you have to sweat over not knowing one of their names (it's even worse if you don't know *either* of their names). Don't you just hate that? Guaranteed bad impression, whether it's business, social, friendship, your friend's husband, anyone.

How much better would your relationships be with people if you were somebody who was consistently excellent with names? I wrote most of this book in a coffee shop in Sydney, Australia, called the Zeebra Café. On my second visit, the owner, Wandi, asked me my name. Ever since, he has greeted me daily by name, and asked me how I am. I can't tell you how special and valued a customer that makes me feel when I see how many people go into his café every day. He only heard my name once, but remembered it forever, and showed me that he really valued me and my custom.

How much more persuasive could you be if you were someone who understood *how* and *when* to use the 'sweetest and most important sound in any language'. If you were one of the ones who even remembers the pet dog's name – imagine what an impact that will have on a business contact or acquaintance that you've only met once or twice.

When you remember and use someone's name, you show them respect and that you are interested enough in them to make an effort to learn their name. And it takes way less than a minute to remember it forever.

Easy name-recall technique

As discussed in Chapter 2, Write beautifully persuasive emails, your brain has three main ways of processing information:

▶▶ *Auditory*

▶▶ *Visual*

▶▶ *Physical, which refers to touch and feel*

(The senses of smell and taste are not so relevant here; I've always thought it's not so cool to try and taste somebody when you first meet them. Mind you, *they'd* probably remember *your* name.)

We use these senses all the time, separately, together and in combination. When you wish to remember somebody's name, the most effective way is to tell it to your brain using all three main representative systems, using the hearing way, the seeing way and then the touchy-feely, physical way. You're going to bombard your senses with an assault of powerful information that will mean it's impossible to forget this name.

▶▶ *The 'hearing' link to the brain comes first, as that's required first when you meet somebody. Say their name back to them immediately they've said it. Then say it to yourself three times.* (That didn't take long, did it?)

▶▶ *The 'seeing' bit comes next. When you are introduced to the person, you need to make a quick link between the way they look and their name. It doesn't matter how tenuous the link is. Often it can be a link between the way they look and the way somebody else looks who has the same name. They might be called Brad and have a chin which looks a little like Brad Pitt's chin. Or they might be called Lucy and have similar blonde hair to another friend of yours called Lucy.* (Just a few seconds)

▶▶ *Finally, the physical connection. Using tiny movements, imagine holding a pen and, whilst looking at them and talking to them, simulate writing the person's name. With imperceptibly small movements, feel yourself writing out that person's name.* (Less than 1 minute for all three steps)

HINTS

■ Somebody introduces themselves to you. 'Hi, I'm Kim.' You say something like, 'Great, nice to meet you, Kim.' Repeating her name. Then to yourself, three times, you say, 'Kim, Kim, Kim.' That's the hearing bit done.

■ Now the visual part. Hmmm. You look at her hair. Guess what, it doesn't really look anything like reality star Kim Kardashian but, hang on, it is about the same length as Kim Kardashian's hair. That'll do. There you go, you've made the connection between this Kim and another Kim. The visual link can be as tenuous as you like, just so long as you actually make it.

■ Then using tiny movements, you imagine holding a pen and write out 'Kim' whilst looking and talking to her. Obviously you don't need to let her see what you're doing, in fact that might make you look a bit weird. This final short act is even more powerful, as you're combining it with the visual trigger of looking at her face at the same time.

■ It's a few months before you see Kim again. But the moment you meet you remember – 'Kim! How are you?' She looks surprised and delighted that you've remembered her name.

One of the good things about the easy name-recall technique is that your brain really has no choice but to remember the name. You are bombarding your brain so effectively, using all the different senses so efficiently, that the easiest thing your brain can do is remember it. You must do it with the three senses. First the hearing connection. Then the seeing connection. Then the physical connection.

One more thing. When I first started doing this, I kept a book with the names of everyone I met in it too. I must admit it did help – the added benefit of writing it down (and the act of telling myself that I had to remember it because I needed to write it down) made a big difference. Keep a book too if you think it will help.

The easy way to diffuse an argument and get your way (also known as 'The Barack Obama TV interview strategy')

Politicians know all about the sweet, sweet sound of a name. And many of them are effective at using it to evade a grilling on difficult issues. Here's something that might make the next time you're watching a boring political interview (slightly) more interesting. Watch for the politician who's receiving a grilling but then subtly uses the first name of the interviewer in reply to a tough question. This often results in the interviewer softening his line of questioning. Why? You already know about the power and compliment of using somebody's name. But there's something else. In this instance, the use of a name perhaps appeals to the deep-seated human feeling that we owe people something when we are given 'a gift' or made a concession. When we are given something, we feel the urge to reciprocate in some way. In this instance – the politician's use of the interviewer's name is the 'gift' or the concession, and the subtly increased respect and intimacy is the returned favour.

I've often watched Barack Obama (and it has to be said, many other politicians) use this. Observe how he carefully adds the anchor's name to his answers. What's particularly impressive is that he doesn't overdo it, and he often waits until a tough question to use it.

'I'm not prepared to make a hard and fast commitment here with you today, John.'

'No, I — actually, let — let me be clear, Brian. I didn't walk it back at all.'

'No. Hold on a second, Bill ... Bill, what I've said is – I've already said it succeeded beyond our wildest dreams ... We are still spending, Bill.'

(Obama interviews with CNBC's John Harwood, NBC Nightly News anchor Brian Williams and Bill O'Reilly of Fox News.)

The effect can often be that the interviewee will react to the 'gift' by softening his line of questioning or indeed move on to something less controversial. The final example above is taken from a transcript of a Fox News interview with

Bill O'Reilly. Obama uses O'Reilly's first name three times. Almost immediately afterwards, a previously aggressive O'Reilly both moves on to a different subject matter and compliments Obama on a good speech he'd recently made.

You can use this knowledge both ways in an argument. Use a name in an argument as a subtle 'gift', a concession that doesn't actually concede any ground on the issue. And if somebody starts using *your* name, notice how it makes you feel. Sometimes you might need to use this knowledge to defend yourself against this effective persuasion strategy and guard against allowing yourself to be swayed from your point of view by flattery.

David's boss Ralph was obviously a very charming and personable man and his talent for remembering names one significant part of his overall charisma. And in the way he dealt with difficult situations at work, it's clear his liberal and intelligent use of that sweet, sweet sound helped him to win arguments as well as friends.

TO-DO LIST: REMINDERS

▶▶ **Easy name recall.** Start using the sweet, sweet sound that people love to hear more than any other. When you first meet somebody, say their name back to them immediately they've said it. Then say it to yourself three times.

Then make a brief link between the way they look and their name. It doesn't matter how tenuous the link is. Often it can be a link between the way they look and the way somebody else of the same name looks. See the Hint box on page 72 for examples.

Finally, the physical connection. Using tiny movements, imagine holding a pen and, whilst looking at and talking to the person, simulate writing their name. With imperceptibly small movements, feel yourself writing out that **person's name.** (Less than a minute for the whole easy-name-recall-technique)

▶▶ **Use names to diffuse an argument or conflict when you want to win a concession or avoid difficult questions.** This acts as a 'gift' that may be reciprocated with a more significant concession from the other person.

CHAPTER 8

Amazing research to help you climb the career ladder

Ali had been pushing really hard in his career for years but he never quite felt like he had made it. He had been with his company for a long time in a role where he was in charge of others but had been stuck in the same job without a promotion for years.

He had the talent, he knew it. He had the drive; he certainly wanted to get to the top. But he'd never quite made those deep connections at work and properly related to the people around him.

He seemed to clash with his team quite a lot. They didn't like receiving his feedback and got very defensive when he had to tell them off. And it wasn't just with his team, he didn't quite gel with the top executives either. When he went into work, he knew he didn't quite have those workplace relationships that others had. He'd

arrive and his boss would be talking animatedly to his colleagues about the football results but all Ali would get was a brief nod of greeting, before the boss turned away to talk to the others again.

How could he persuade his employers to like him? And how could he persuade his team to not be so defensive when he gave them feedback?

A high percentage of successful people agree on one specific area that has helped them achieve the level of success that they have.

In 2008 I decided to make a new range of audiobooks that were simply interviews with successful people. One was called *How to Make Money*, which was how I found myself in a café in central London sitting opposite a multi-millionaire. In fact in one week I'd been lucky enough to meet four different millionaire businessmen. I asked each of them the same question.

'What is the secret of your success?'

And the answer this particular wealthy guy gave amazed me. The reason I was so amazed was that his answer was *the same* as the other three. It was also the same as many, if not most, of the top people I'd met in business, sport, entertainment and music. How could I not have been aware that this one trait apparently had so much significance?

What was it then? What was that common factor? All four millionaires I spoke to that week responded identically. 'Relationships,' they said.

They regarded the secret of their success to be the quality and depth of the personal relationships they have in their professional lives, which of course in turn means others will be more receptive to them, their message and their talents. Here are a few quotes from those interviews:

'I believe deeply in relationships. Knowing people is 50 per cent of this business.'

'Being really good friends with people and getting to know people I work with is key.'

'Not only build those relationships and network but keep in contact with people.'

'I have to really like the people that I work with and if I like the people that I work with I want to do well for them.'

'My relationships with people that have been from over a couple of decades have come back to be of value to me. Often when they have been long forgotten.'

So, how do you build and maintain these relationships?

I present to you five amazing and fun bits of persuasion research that can help you build and maintain those vital working relationships.

▶▶ *How to deliver any message under the radar*
▶▶ *Leave the flares and the corduroy jacket at home*
▶▶ *The persuasion science behind making a cup of tea*
▶▶ *Learn when to complain and when to shut up*
▶▶ *The slightly unpleasant tasting hamburger*

How to deliver any message under the radar

'You guys are useless and you need to work a lot harder if you're going to stay at this company.'

Ben's audience simply smiled as though in a slight trance. It was breathtaking. As the most junior employee in the small meeting room, Ben had just directly insulted an audience of six people who were all at least ten years his senior within the company. How could he get away with being so rude to his superiors?

For the answer, let's go back to the embedded commands from Chapter 2, Write beautifully persuasive emails. For a truly effective way to get any message in under the radar, move on a step from embedded commands to embedded quotations. Sometimes you have to deliver a tough message in the workplace, and it's hard to do it without offending. You can do so with an embedded quotation.

▶▶ *Come up with a story, or tale, or statement and put your suggestion in a quotation. Your message gets in under the radar because your audience isn't on conscious alert for it. It slips straight under the radar.* (1 minute for story and message)

It works because the 'message' comes from a character in your story. You couldn't possibly take the consequences for that, could you?

John Grindler and Richard Bandler invented NLP together, a series of theories and concepts on how to communicate better with yourself and other people. They say in their book *Frogs Into Princes*, 'You can try any new behavior in quotes and it won't seem to be you doing it.' They give a perfect example that shows how much fun you can have with quotes. 'I can go into a restaurant and walk up to a waitress and say, "I just went in the bathroom and this guy walked up to me and said 'Blink', and find out what happens. She'll blink and I'll go, 'Isn't that weird?' and walk away."'

Embedded commands can change beliefs and behaviour, and often people will be unaware that this has immediately occurred at a conscious level. And it can be any message you want to sneak in under the radar, such as feeling good, learning quickly, following someone's lead, acting quickly, whatever your imagination can come up with.

An old teacher of mine told me, 'Learn this stuff and it'll have a huge impact on your work', and indeed it has. *

Leave the flares and the corduroy jacket at home

Yup, piece of research number two says what you wear directly affects your ability to build and maintain relationships at work. There are two separate clothing approaches here. Sadly, neither of them is likely to incorporate the knitted jumper that Granny gave you at Christmas.

---

* I'm sure you spotted my gratuitous use of an embedded quotation here. There are a number of others in this chapter, can you spot them? And then start to deliver your own messages under the radar.

Do you want to be the equal of someone you're trying to establish a relationship with or have authority over them?

Wardrobe 1

Rapport helps you to get your way. Author Gene Z. Laborde gives us a stark warning of what will happen if we don't get rapport in the workplace. He says, 'Without rapport, you will not get what you want – not money, not promotions, not friends.' You can get rapport by 'mirroring' or 'matching' other people, and one fairly easily way to do this is by dressing similarly to others. If you want to build trust and liking with your co-workers, build rapport by dressing similarly.

Sadly this approach doesn't say much for the individual in us just bursting to express their creativity, but if it means leaving the 'ironic' 1980s denim jumpsuit in the wardrobe, then maybe that's just as well.

OBVIOUS FOOTNOTE: Actually wearing *identical* clothes as other people is likely to really hack them off. As with all other areas of rapport, the aim is to be similar, not identical.

Wardrobe 2

Authority helps you to get your way. By dressing more smartly than your audience, the research suggests you gain authority, and therefore increase your persuasiveness.

A few years ago, three researchers called Khan, Chawla and Devine asked almost a thousand small business owners a number of questions about accountants. At this point I'd forgive you for thinking this survey sounds a little dull, but bear with me. The small business owners were asked to rank a number of accountants on likelihood of hiring, expertise, knowledge, trustworthiness, credibility, reliability, professionalism, friendliness and honesty. In almost all the categories, the smartly dressed accountants scored much higher than the casual ones. In other words, dress more smartly, and score higher on trustworthiness, credibility, reliability, professionalism, friendliness and honesty. In addition, our old friend the persuasion researcher Nicolas Gueguen turned his attention from busty hitchhikers to jaywalkers. He found that five times as many people followed a jaywalker in a suit across a busy street as opposed to a poorly dressed jaywalker.

In their book *You Need This Book To Get What You Want*, Scott Solder and Mark Noble advise to dress 'one-notch above everyone else' if making a presentation. Normally good advice, but I think there are a few exceptions. Motivational speaker Tony Robbins often goes on stage wearing shorts and trainers, and having witnessed his impressive 'Unleash the Power' seminars I can confirm he has total and utter authority.

One thing's for certain; all this means that whether you are aiming for rapport, authority or compliance, there is sadly no room for your flares and corduroy jacket at work. Unless, of course, everyone else at your workplace is wearing flares and a corduroy jacket...

The persuasion science behind making a cup of tea

A friend of mine is a TV presenter in the UK and we were out celebrating his top new gig. No doubt about it, this one was a big step up for him and he was delighted. While we were out, his agent called.

> 'It's your first day in the office on Monday – go and make the tea for everyone.'
>
> 'Eh?'
>
> 'You heard me, just make a round of teas for the people you work with. You'll see.'
>
> 'Okay, okay.'
>
> Two days later, I saw my friend again. He was buzzing.
>
> 'Wow – that really worked. About half eleven, I offered to make everyone a cup of tea, and they seemed to warm to me much more after that. One even commented that the previous presenter would never have done that.'

There've been numerous studies to prove that when we give people something, we're more likely to get something back. Shoppers who've been given a free sample are more likely to buy a product. Your colleague is more likely to invite you to a party if you've already invited him to one of yours. Waiters are more likely to get a tip when they leave a little sweet on the table next to the bill.

The cup of tea is just another gift, and in return you're getting people's trust and approval (as well as, hopefully, a few cups of tea made for you in the future!).

Studies suggest that when you give somebody something small, they feel an unconscious desire to reciprocate by giving something back, even if it's a whole lot bigger.

Cup of tea = some great in-office PR that money can't buy.

Even if the coffee machine is free or you're simply boiling the kettle, your gift is the time and effort it takes to go and fetch the drinks.

Bosses please note: the rest of us like it when *you* occasionally make the teas too.

▶▶ *Give a little gift, and build relationships.* *(1 minute to boil the kettle)*

Learn when to complain and when to shut up

Nobody likes a moaner right? Who wants to work with someone who complains a lot, or who's constantly whingeing about stuff they're not happy with?

Actually research suggests that complaining and expressing negativity doesn't always have a negative impact on building relationships.

When you don't know someone at work that well, the research suggests it's good to be positive and hide negative thoughts and feelings. But when you already get on well with someone, being relentlessly positive isn't so important. Researchers Linda Tickle-Degnen and Robert Rosenthal found in a study that people don't mind their work friends having a grumble 'because they would have had a history of positive behaviour in earlier interactions'. And researchers at New Zealand's Victoria University of Wellington found that whingeing or whining described as a 'long or repeated expression of discontent' was actually a helpful way of building more rapport.

Interestingly, the same research suggests it's even better if you swear a bit in this big workplace rant. However, persuasion author Richard M. Perloff says that in many instances 'obscene speech is risky, it violates audience expectations of what is appropriate.'

So when you've already got rapport, research suggests the odd conspiratorial whinge can actually help to build relationships. We all have an off day, and this research proves that even when things aren't going so well you can use it to your advantage. But be careful not to moan too much...

The slightly unpleasant tasting hamburger

A 2004 study on workplaces published in the *American Behavioral Scientist* and quoted in the *Wall Street Journal* found that 'Teams with buoyant moods who encouraged each other earned higher profits and better customer satisfaction ratings.'

Well, duh. Exactly as you'd expect, right? Except the problem is that research shows fewer of us are happy at work than ever before. Indeed this problem is being taken so seriously in the States that happiness coaches are being brought in to lift people's spirits. One of their suggestions, apparently, is to send an email to your co-workers every day thanking them for something they've done. (I've worked at places where some of my colleagues would have thought I'd gone mad if I sent such an email!)

Sometimes though, a tricky workplace situation comes up, and something simply needs to be said. When you want to deliver some negative feedback to someone at work, use the hamburger approach. As an old boss of mine used to say, 'Make sure your target "digests" the unpleasant bit by putting the criticism in a fluffy light bun of positivity.'

Something positive (*light fluffy bun*)
The meat of the issue (*unpleasant tasting hamburger*)
Something else positive (*light fluffy bun*)

HINT

■ Here's an example of the slightly unpleasant tasting hamburger.

Hi Pete,

You did a great job on the report you put together. I particularly liked the example at the start. The paragraph on revenue streams needs to be stronger though and you could do with backing it up with some figures. Other than that though, it's a great piece of work. Well done.

■ And here's another slightly more informal example.

Tom, well done today. Your team got the work done very effectively. However, I must say it didn't go down very well when you used the line 'You look like a blueberry' to James. I don't think he's seen the film *Anchorman* and may have been offended by it. Maybe quote from *Top Gun* next time. But, overall, great job!

It's a respect thing. People talk to each other at work in a very different way to how they would talk to one another in any other situation. It's easy to criticise, but how are you delivering that criticism?

Ali had been pushing really hard in his career, but never quite felt like he'd made it to the level he deserved. When I told him about the slightly unpleasant tasting hamburger, his response was serious. 'I don't have time to sugar coat every piece of criticism throughout a working day.' That's fair enough. But the truth is that people like praise, not criticism. And in the days and weeks after we spoke Ali thought more about it, and slowly started to change the way he delivered feedback. He started to notice a change in how his team responded to him on a personal level.

As the research illustrates, happy teams increase profits and customer satisfaction, so why wouldn't you serve up a slightly unpleasant tasting hamburger?

TO-DO LIST: REMINDERS

A high percentage of successful people regard the secret of their success to be the quality and depth of their relationships: the personal relationships they have in their professional lives that have helped them to climb the ladder. Follow these five steps to build solid and lasting relationships:

▶▶ How to deliver any message under the radar.

▶▶ Leave the flares and the corduroy jacket at home.

▶▶ The persuasion science behind making a cup of tea.

▶▶ Learn when to complain and when to shut up.

▶▶ The slightly unpleasant tasting hamburger.

CHAPTER 9

Persuasive presentations

Elizabeth would happily admit it – she didn't enjoy presentations. It was normally only to two or three clients, but she really didn't like them. It wasn't that she felt 'pukey and anxious' before them, more that she knew she didn't actually make much of an impact.

'It's not that I'm nervous, I just hate, hate, hate making presentations.'

In person and in a one-on-one situation, Elizabeth was really engaging, but when it came to small work presentations, this didn't come across. Her voice was naturally quite high, which possibly didn't help, and when she needed to convey authority, she knew that she simply didn't do it very well. To make things worse, she regularly seemed to get slightly lost with her notes, which slowed everything down.

She'd been to presentations where people felt totally relaxed, laughed lots, had a good time and came out

really enthusiastic about what they'd just seen. People didn't do this after watching her, though.

By presentations, I'm talking about any situation where you are presenting an idea and attempting to persuade somebody of your point of view. It might be a pitch, a speech, a demonstration, a social evening, book club, or just a chat with friends. In particular, you might be trying to close a deal or make the case for something important in a meeting.

This chapter deals with general presentation strategies to make your audience more open, receptive and compliant. And then it combines well with the specifics in the final chapter, Close the deal.

▶▶ *Stage 1. Preparation: make your presentation twice as good*
▶▶ *Stage 2. Take them to a different place*
▶▶ *Stage 3. Tell stories*
▶▶ *Stage 4. Tell them what not to do*
▶▶ *Stage 5. The sound of authority*
▶▶ *Stage 6. Closing the deal*

Stage 1. Preparation: make your presentation twice as good

Ditch the notes. The way to make a connection with people is not by burying your head in a sheaf of paper or having your audience looking at a screen rather than you. That may mean ditching the PowerPoint too. To present properly, you need to look into people's eyes and tell them what you think.

Even more importantly, you need to use your eyes to register how your audience is reacting to your presentation, whether it is one person or upwards of 100 people. If you stumble over a word, that's fine. Nobody cares. If you don't look them in the eye because you're fiddling with the projector or reading something out word for word, you miss the chance to register how they're reacting.

I've worked in TV and radio making different kinds of presentations for years. If you are somebody who gets nervous, the following steps will ensure your presentation is as outstanding and persuasive as possible:

1. *Prepare on as many pieces of paper as you like. Be as detailed as you like.*
2. *Then shrink it down to bullet points so it fits on a small piece of paper (ideally Post-it note size). (1 minute)*
3. *Record selected sections of your presentation on a recording device, one minute at a time (phone, laptop, iPod, anything). When you make a mistake, stop (but don't stop recording) and go back over the same sentence until you get that particular minute absolutely right. When you don't sound as persuasive as you'd like to sound, again, stop (but don't stop recording) and go back over the same sentence until you get it right. (1 minute per section)*
4. *Listen back. Do this on the day of your presentation.*

It is the stopping after a mistake and recording correctly that seems to work so effectively. On a conscious level, you become aware of the parts of your presentation you haven't got totally sorted yet. On a deeper level, you are sending a strong message to your sub-conscious to listen out for key points in the speech that you're not totally comfortable with, and rehearsing these until you get it right. In this way, you're dealing with challenges before they happen.

If your presentation is more of a two-way conversation or chat, that's fine. Just record the bits you can, and listen back. Work on what you can control. It'll make a big difference.

Stage 2. Take them to a different place

I was at a magic show in central London and a strange thing was happening. The magician was doing something very cool with his audience. Whenever he walked to a specific part of the stage, inexplicably the audience started laughing at his corny jokes. Whenever he returned to that spot, we (yes, me included) had that same funny, happy feeling, even if he wasn't delivering a punchline.

When he moved to a different part of the stage, the suspense would mysteriously grow and people seemed to become quiet and intense. How on earth could the simple act of a magician standing in a certain place make a whole audience feel a different way?

The magician had been doing something very simple. At the start of his show, every time he told a joke he would move to a specific spot as he delivered the punchline. After a while he could move there without telling a joke and the audience would … still laugh.

The magician was using what's called 'spatial anchoring'. The idea originates from Pavlov and his sneaky experiments with dogs. Every time he fed the dogs, he would ring a bell. After a while, when he rang a bell, the dogs would salivate even if there was no food – the bell became an 'anchor'. You can use anchors to make yourself feel better, and you can use them to influence other people too. They can be particularly useful in a presentation setting. Be warned: this is good fun.

▶▶ *Think of a way you'd like your audience to feel. Move into a particular space and make them feel like that (through stories, anecdotes, questions, statements, etc.). Repeat this process as many times as possible until you notice how it works whenever you move to the place. (1 minute max in the space)*

As when Pavlov rung the bell and the dogs started to salivate, now when you move into the different place, your audience will feel the way you want them to. Simple.

How can you use this in a presentation?

- Set up a place for 'questions'. Whenever you stand in a certain spot, you ask for questions. After a while, people associate that spot with questions. Whenever you stand there, it means you want interaction.
- Set up a place for 'feeling good'. If you only deliver good news or tell stories about feeling good when you are

sitting down, after a while, your audience will associate you sitting down with ... feeling good.

- Set up a place for 'feeling decisive'. Likewise, when it comes to decision time, you can have a place established where people already feel decisive. Because every time you've sat/stood there, you've got them to associate with that emotional experience.

Occupy a different place, and take your audience into a different place too.

Stage 3. Tell them stories

Take a look back over the previous stage and the story of the magic show in central London. I could have simply told you the technique. Instead, I told you the story of someone who did it themselves, so you could see exactly how the technique works in a practical setting.

▶▶ *Get your point across by telling a story about what you want your audience to do.* (1 minute)

How could you make a dry presentation more exciting with a story or a metaphor? Can you ditch the stats and incorporate instead a tale to illustrate your point? A story about an investor who made their millions by taking a risk on a company just like yours? Or a football team that won their league after doing extra training? Your message will be in the story, and you can make that message as subtle or unsubtle as you like.

I want you to make your presentations special and unique to your audience, and perhaps the best way to do this is to illustrate how someone else does it. We all like hearing a story, so as soon as you say to someone 'Let me tell you a story', you'll have their interest. Guaranteed.

Stage 4. Tell them what *not* to do

If I tell you: 'Don't think about a pink car', what do you instantly think about? The way the brain works, we have to process what a pink car looks like before we can work out not to think about it. It works every time. Imagine if you were to say to a child:

'Please, please, please don't consider how happy you would be if I were to get a cute little fluffy puppy for you to keep.'

If you weren't actually intending on getting a cute little fluffy puppy, that'd be SO cruel, wouldn't it? Because, of course, the child will think about that cute little fluffy puppy, despite having been told not to.

You can tell your audience what you're 'not going to do' and be subtly persuasive with this language trick.

▶▶ *Tell your audience what to do, by actually telling them what not to do.* (1 minute)

HINT

■ Here are some examples.

'I don't want you to consider buying this just yet...'

'Don't think about how this might benefit you until I've told you all about the extra features.'

'Please don't sign the petition until you've heard all sides of the argument.'

'I'm not going to ask you to sign off this proposal just now...'

'You shouldn't take my word for it without considering the evidence...'

■ And you *shouldn't* start using this in your presentations until you've found your own way of making it work for you.

Stage 5. The sound of authority

There's been a lot written about the role of authority in persuasion – about establishing yourself as the authority figure by discreetly detailing your experience and credentials. Indeed it is one of Dr Robert Cialdini's widely respected six 'weapons of influence'. But when it comes to a presentation, simply the way you sound can have a massive impact on your persuasiveness.

Your voice quickly demonstrates whether you have that effortless command and control of the situation that we associate with authoritative presenters.

From my years of experience as a presenter on TV and radio, I would say that those who speak with a lower tone and slightly slower, more deliberate pace tend to convey a more authoritative tone. Higher and faster is more childlike (and, some research suggests, submissive). But here we hit a problem. It's all very well saying a lower voice is more authoritative and persuasive, but you can't just magically make your voice a lot lower. I think most people sound a bit odd when they start doing that.

Here's a way to get that sound of authority easily, whilst still being 'you'. When our voice goes up at the end of a sentence, it becomes a question. When we stay level at the end of a sentence, it is a statement. When we go down, it becomes a command. When you focus on very small, key parts of your presentation like this, it can be the difference between wrapping it up successfully or not.

HINT

- Imagine the sentence, 'Tidy your room.' Try it all three ways. First go up at the end of the sentence. Then stay level. Then go down. Sounds different, right?

  - Upward inflection at end of sentence = question.

  - Level inflection at end of sentence = statement.

  - Downward inflection at end of sentence = command.

- Use this in your presentations to deliver key lines in an authoritative way. You're not trying to lower your voice all the way through your speech; you're making key sentences more persuasive with respectful authority by using downward inflection.

- How do the following sentences sound with upward inflection, and then downward?

  'Would you like to make me an offer?'

  'We'd like you to invest £15,000 in our company.'

  'I wonder if you'd like to sign up now.'

As you can see, you can have fun with this too. All these work even better with the 'softeners' discussed in Chapter 2, Write beautifully persuasive emails.

Elizabeth's voice was naturally quite high, and she was aware of it, even quite self-conscious. However, whenever she'd tried to do anything about it she'd found it almost impossibly hard to focus on her voice and what she was saying at the same time. So she started focusing on two key sentences in the normal presentation she made to deliver these with more authority, a bit slower and using downward tonality at the end. She got used to this quite quickly. And then she was able to extend these techniques to more parts of her speech, making her sound more in control and more authoritative. Oh, and she also ditched the notes.

Stage 6. Closing the deal

This chapter deals with general presentational persuasion strategies to make your audience open to what you have to say. Hopefully, like Elizabeth, you've already started to make changes to appear and sound much more persuasive. Your audience is ready to listen and accept your ideas.

Now you want to wrap things up with some specifics. As you are looking to be persuasive, end your meeting with a suitable close, a call to action or a summary.

What is your call to action? That's why the 'close the deal' section comes next. It concentrates on a number of strategies for getting people to say yes. So go there now, pick the relevant technique and use it in your presentation.

TO-DO LIST: REMINDERS

Preparation. Record small chunks of your presentation beforehand. When you make a mistake, stop (but don't stop recording) and go back over the same sentence until you get it right. This will make your presentation twice as good. (1 minute)

Take them to a different place by 'anchoring' a specific positive emotion in a particular area. (1 minute)

Tell stories and make your presentation special and unique. (1 minute)

Tell your audience what to do by telling them what not to do. (Max 1 minute)

Authority. Focus on delivering key sentences in your presentation with more authority, by speaking slower and with downward inflection on key 'commands'. (1 minute)

When you're ready to ***close the deal***, move to the next chapter.

CHAPTER 10

Close the deal

Alex gets frustrated. He works in sales, but he's not making as much as his colleagues. True, they are some of the best in the business and have been doing it a lot longer than him, but he's just not very good at closing the deal.

Tamara is frustrated too. She's been texting a guy for weeks now, but nothing seems to come of it. She's tried subtly suggesting that they take it a stage further and actually go out on a proper date, but the penny hasn't dropped and he just changed the subject. But ... he still seems keen. Odd. So how does she get him to take action?

And Pete is also frustrated. He has been trying to persuade his friend John to go on holiday with him to Ibiza this summer. He's tried everything. Bribery, photos of girls who will be there, even getting down on both knees and pleading. But John keeps just laughing and saying, 'It sounds awesome, I'll think about it.' Pete really wants to go on this lads' holiday with his friend,

but how does he get him to actually say yes?

Alex, Tamara and Pete all want to hurry things along a little and 'close the deal', but how?

The following techniques can be used in a whole host of different settings, whether it's wrapping up some business, finding a partner or persuading your friend to come on holiday. Heck, you could even use these techniques to sell your car on eBay. Have fun with them and use them honestly. And, to get that all important 'yes', remember to tie in the more general techniques that have appeared earlier in the book.

Now – close the deal by:

▶▶ *Getting them to 'jump on the bandwagon'*
▶▶ *Using 'snob appeal'*
▶▶ *The importance of testimonials*
▶▶ *Putting the clock on it*
▶▶ *If you're struggling, get that foot in the door*
▶▶ *Don't be needy*

Bandwagon technique

This is what the advertising industry refers to when they persuade people to buy something because lots of other people are. Take a look at the cover of this book for an example of 'bandwagon technique': 'The iTunes bestselling author'. I don't tell you that to boast – I tell you because I can use this information as an honest and genuine example of how lots of people buy in to what I do. But the bandwagon technique doesn't just have to be sales-related, you can use it in lots of different situations. Check the Hint box below for examples. The more specific you can be with your bandwagon example, the better. All you do is make it known how popular something is.

▶▶ *At the point you want to close the deal, use the bandwagon technique. Simply make reference to who's already on the bandwagon.* *(1 minute)*

HINT

■ Bandwagon examples:

'James, Laura, Kev and Katie have already said they'll come to the party…'

'Over 100,000 audiobooks sold on iTunes'

'8 out of 10 cats prefer it'

'All my friends at school have got a puppy, why can't we have one too?'

■ And remember, the more specific, the better.

'Pete, Jules, and Sam said how much fun it is', is better than, 'Everybody says how much fun it is.'

Snob appeal

This is the opposite of the bandwagon technique. Snob appeal means that a product is deliberately marketed as something that the mainstream masses would never invest in. For those who do decide to buy it, they are made to feel that they achieve an exclusive status. So by all means use snob appeal rather than the bandwagon technique if it's going to help.

HINT

■ Snob appeal examples:

'Nobody else has this in the UK.'

'You can't even buy this in the shops.'

'This is the first time that this has become available.'

'This costs £2,500 and there are only five of them in the world.'

The importance of testimonials

Have you ever tried to book a hotel in New York? It's unbelievably expensive. The hotel owners in Manhattan have always known they were on to a good thing: millions of visitors, the most valuable real estate in the world and a shortage of hotel rooms have meant they have always charged high, high prices.

But in 2010 hotel owners in New York were hit by a calamity. They realised that life would never be the same again. Why?

Bedbugs.

Tiny little parasitic insects everywhere in New York. It was front-page news. Expensive hotels and cheap hostels. Upmarket and downtown. Flagship department stores such as Niketown, Hollister and Abercrombie and Fitch had to be shut. Even cinema-goers in Times Square were bitten by bedbugs because of a city-wide infestation.

Where does all this fit in with persuasion skills? Well, the hotel industry has changed beyond recognition over the last few years. Pre-internet, all proprietors needed to do was take some photos of their hotel, Photoshop out any bits they didn't want potential guests to see, release a glossy brochure and wait for the bookings to flood in. Us punters would go into a travel agent, say, 'Ooh, that looks nice', and end up disappointed when it wasn't actually the deep-blue sea outside our window but a sewage canal.

Now, we have tripadvisor and all the other hotel review sites that provide honest reviews from other travellers. All the advertising in the world can't hide a few bad reviews on tripadvisor, and once a few becomes a bandwagon, a hotel is in trouble.

When the bedbugs hit New York, international travellers got nervous and hit the web to find out which establishments they were going to get bitten in. Before long, it wasn't just hotel review sites providing the information but specific bedbug review sites had sprung up, such as bedbugregistry. com.

Hotels in New York were therefore forced to treat testimonials as the life or potential death of their business. They did everything to ensure people knew exactly what measures they'd taken to combat the little critters. I recently stayed in New York and it was quite obvious from a brief internet search which hotels still had a problem, which had never had a problem and which (most of them…) had taken serious and extreme measures to make sure that there were absolutely no bedbugs on their premises. (My hotel had a kind of plastic sheet over the mattress and entirely metal furniture. Not particularly comfortable, but no bedbugs.)

The upside to all of this is that testimonials provide honest feedback that forces the provider to think about the product. Ultimately, it forced the hotels to take their customers, and the culture of online testimonials, seriously.

▶▶ *Gather testimonials from others on your product, service, deal, etc. Take the opportunity to really focus on what you are offering and how you can make it great.*

▶▶ *When you want to close the deal, present written/audio/ video testimonials about how outstanding what you have to offer is. (1 minute)*

▶▶ *If in business, ask satisfied customers if you could pass on their details to a potential client. (1 minute)*

I just had an email from an app developer asking about the company that makes my iPhone apps. I was happy to send back a glowing report because it was great to work with this company. That kind of testimonial is probably better than any advertising, just as a bedbug review is *worse* for a hotel than any advertising.

Put the clock on it

At the time of writing, online company Groupon has just been valued at $15 billion. It's a simple concept: a daily email with a massive saving on something in your area. It works because a) it's always a big discount and a great deal, and b) you have to sign up on the day, otherwise the deal is lost.

I recently received a daily email from a similar company for a self-development course in Sydney, reduced from $1,495 to $795. I instantly clicked through and had a look at the deal. I thought about it for an hour, then took action. I paid up. Hmm, almost $800 poorer and it wasn't even lunchtime. There is absolutely no way I would have signed up to the course that day if it wasn't for the fact I had to act there and then to get the big discount. But I'm happy I did. There you have it – the perfect transaction. I had the clock worked on me perfectly – and I was delighted because I got great value. Both sides are happy.

So you want to close the deal. Make them realise that the deal is not going to be there forever. They'd better act fast, otherwise it'll be gone.

▶▶ *Make an offer for a limited time.*

▶▶ *Make your availability limited (or your product, or whatever).*

▶▶ *Set a deadline.*

▶▶ *(You can also limit the quantity of what you're offering.)*

Get a commitment, however small

Remember our friend the persuasion researcher Nicolas Gueguen (he of 'Bust Size and Hitchhiking: A Field Study' fame)? Well, Gueguen did another study in which one 'nice-looking' bloke approached 360 women and asked them if they'd like to have a drink with him. With some, the man simply went up and asked them straight out. But with some, he asked for a smaller commitment first. All he did was ask for directions or for a light, and Gueguen found even that tiny positive commitment was enough to significantly increase the yes factor. Women were more likely to want to go for a drink after the small initial request.

Singles, take note.

Now go back to Chapter 3, Raise more money for charity than you ever dreamed possible, and check out the foot-in-the-door technique again. That's exactly what the 'nice-looking' bloke was doing. In the politest possible way, he was getting his foot-in-the-door by asking for a smaller positive response (commitment) to his request.

How can you use this knowledge if you are struggling to close the deal? By getting a smaller commitment that is in some way related to the bigger commitment you are seeking. In other words – by getting your foot firmly wedged in that door.

▶▶ *If you are struggling to close the deal, gain a smaller commitment before leaving the communication. Like this: 'If you don't want to buy now, would you be happy to commit to another meeting in a week's time to further explore these proposals?'* (1 minute)

Conclusion: It's harder to say no, when you've already said yes.

Don't be needy

This might be one of the most important points in the book. Remember Herb Cohen, the ace negotiator? I want to remind you once again of his quote (see Chapter 5, Get that pay rise).

'You should care, really care ... but not t-h-a-t much.'

Whether it's the salesman who wants to sell you a car so badly he's on his knees or the prospective date who has left you twenty-three phone messages, when somebody cares too much it's a turn-off.

Herb Cohen goes on to say that the best way to make a good deal is to convey to the other side, 'I can live without this deal'.

Make yourself valuable and demonstrate confidence and self-respect with your attitude. Care, but not that much. As

James Lloyd, author of the audiobook *Persuasion Secrets*, says, 'People who know they'll be okay if they are turned down are less likely to be turned down.'

Back to Tamara. She'd tried to ask 'the guy' out and he'd basically ignored her. But they still had this weird text relationship going. Was he all text and no action? She put the clock on him. She simply sent him an SMS that read, 'I'm going to LA for a month next week. So you'd better hurry up and ask me out otherwise you'll lose your chance.' As soon as Tamara put the clock on it, the guy realised that he might miss his chance. He promptly asked her out.

Pete had been trying to persuade his mate to come on holiday to Ibiza with him. His friend was keen but wouldn't commit. In the end Pete asked some other friends to come (he *really* wanted that holiday!). His other friends had been the year before and had had a brilliant time, so said yes. Pete had unwittingly started to activate the bandwagon technique, because as soon as John heard the others were coming, he became more interested. He spoke to the other friends, who provided a powerful testimonial of what a great time they'd had the year before. The bandwagon technique, combined with the testimonial, was enough to get John to book too.

And what about Alex, the failing salesman? Well, he didn't actually change that much. He just got a bit less desperate. He got a sense of perspective and had a bit more fun. *He cared … but not that much*. He knew that one way or the other, 'it'd be okay'. As a consequence, clients seemed to like him more. Sometimes that meant a sale and sometimes it didn't, and it was a whole lot more fun having that attitude.

TO-DO LIST: REMINDERS

Bandwagon technique. At the point you want to close the deal, use the bandwagon technique. Make reference to who's already doing it and how much they're loving it. (1 minute)

Snob appeal. Alternatively, try this approach whereby a product is deliberately marketed as something that the masses would never buy. For those who do invest in it, they achieve status and exclusivity. (1 minute)

Testimonials. Present powerful written/audio/video testimonials on how great your offering is. (1 minute)

Put the clock on it. Make your offer limited by 'putting the clock on it'. Remember how I spent $800 in a morning? Make an offer for a limited time, make your availability limited and/or set a deadline. (Max 1 minute)

Foot in the door. If you are struggling to close the deal, focus on getting a smaller but related commitment. That smaller commitment can lead to a bigger one in future. (1 minute)

Don't be needy. Make yourself and your time valuable, and act with confidence and self-respect.

Final bit

As a final thought, what if all else is failing? What if they just don't want to be persuaded?

Well, maybe it's you who has to shift your position.

You can't persuade anyone to do something if they simply don't want to do it. They won't allow it. So maybe you just have to improve what you're offering. Or see it from their point of view.

If they won't budge and they won't change their mind, it's time to put yourself in their shoes. What makes them feel so strongly about this issue, and do they have a valid point? Perhaps you need to persuade *yourself* of *their* argument.

▶▶ See, hear and feel your argument from their point of view. What are their objections? How can you address them?
(1 minute)

Having the ability to listen and compromise is as important a persuasion tool as any other in this book. Because the easiest way to influence people is by giving them what they want.

Acknowledgements

I am very grateful to everyone who's helped in the putting together of *Persuade in a Minute*. In particular:

Thanks to Rich Sweetman for his thoughts and assistance with Chapter 4, How to make the most of Facebook. (His status updates are still cheesy but very persuasive.) Also thank you to all the Facebook friends that I roped into various experiments for this chapter. Big 'Like' to you all.

Thanks to James Mooring for his assistance with Chapter 5, Get that pay rise, and to both James and Cor for their wonderful hospitality in Australia while I wrote much of this book. It was also James who introduced me to daily deal sites (Chapter 10) and ensured I was $800 dollars poorer before lunchtime.

Special thanks to all the mums, dads and kids I spoke to for Chapter 6, How to get a seven-year-old to tidy their room. In particular, supermums Aurelie Kennedy, Annette Twigg, Samantha Hodgson, Lena Hammond, and Sally Warburton. And extra special thanks to my friend and ex-co-presenter on Atlantic 252, Becky Chippindale (the one who took the chocolate buttons away), for doing further research with her army of (yummy) mummys.

Thanks to John Hirst and Quentin Hunt for their assistance and advice on Chapter 9, Persuasive presentations. They are indeed both very persuasive presenters.

Thanks to 'queen of grammar' Sherry Abuel-Ealeh for her help, and Lori Smale for taking time out from abusing me on Twitter to read through and offer her thoughts.

Thanks to my agents Andy Hipkiss at Triple A Media and James Wills at Watson Little who continue to provide brilliant support. Thanks to Zoe Howes and Jenni Lewis for their help with the audiobook version (available on iTunes now!) and thanks to Kasi Collins and Jenny Rowley for being excellent (and persuasive) publicists.

Finally, thanks to my editor Clare Wallis at Virgin Books for being brilliant to work with. And patient too...

Bibliography

Arbuthnot, J., Tedeschi, R., Wayner, M., Turner, J., Kressler, S. and Rush, R., 'The Induction of Sustained Recycling Behavior Through The Foot-in-the-Door Technique', *Journal of Environmental Systems* (1976-77).

Bandler, R. and Grinder, J., Frogs into Princes: *Neuro Linguistic Programming*, Real People Press (1979).

Carnegie, Dale, *How To Win Friends and Influence People*, Simon and Schuster (1936).

Cialdini, Dr Robert, *Influence: The Psychology of Persuasion*, Collins, (1984).

Cohen, Herb, *Outlines and Ideas about Selling and Negotiating*, available online from herbcohenonline.com

Daly, N., Holmes, J., Newton, J. and Stubbe, M., 'Expletives as Solidarity Signals in FTAs on the Factory Floor', available online from www.sciencedirect.com (2003).

Gladwell, Malcolm, *The Tipping Point: How Little Things Can Make a Big Difference*, Abacus, new edition (2001).

Guéguen, Nicolas, 'Bust Size and Hitchhiking: A Field Study', *Perceptual and Motor Skills*, (2007).

Guéguen, N. and Jacob, C., 'The Effect of Touch on Tipping: An Evaluation in a French Bar', available online from *Université Européenne de Bretagne* (2007).

Guéguen N., Marchand M., Pascual A. and Lourel M., 'Foot-in-the-Door Technique Using a Courtship Request: A Field Experiment', *Psychol Rep*, (2008).

Khan, Z. U., Chawla, S. K. and Devine, E. A., 'Impact of Gender, Race, and Dress on Choice of CPA's,' *Journal of Applied Business Research* (1996-1997).

Laborde, Gene Z., *Influencing with Integrity: Management Skills for Communication and Negotiation*, Crown House Publishing (1984).

Langer, E., Blank, A. and Chanowitz, B., 'The Mindlessness of Ostensibly Thoughtful Action: The Role of "Placebic" Information in Interpersonal Interaction', available online from *Journal of Personality and Social Psychology* (1978).

Lloyd, James, *Persuasion Secrets*, available on iTunes from Puttenham Limited, (2009).

Perloff, Richard, M., *The Dynamics of Persuasion: Communication and Attitudes in the 21st Century*. Routledge (2007).

Schwarzwald, J., Bizman, A. and Raz, M., 'The Foot-in-the-Door Paradigm: Effects of a Second Request Size on Donation Probability and Donor Generosity', *Personality and Social Psychology Bulletin*, (1983).

Shellenbarger, Sue, 'Thinking Happy Thoughts at Work', *Wall Street Journal*, (2010).

Smart,J, 'Jamie Smart's NLP Tip - Tip #196 - The Secret Language of Influence - Part 3 - Covert Influence Techniques', available online.

Solder, S. and Noble, M., *You Need This Book to Get What You Want*, Simon and Schuster (2010).

Taylor, T. and Booth-Butterfield, S., 'Getting a Foot in the Door with Drinking and Driving: A Field Study of Healthy Influence', *Communication Research Reports*, (1993).

Tickle-Degnen, L. and Rosenthal, R., 'The Nature of Rapport and Its Nonverbal Correlates', available online from *Psychological Inquiry* (1990).

Weber, Thomas, E. *Cracking the Facebook Code*, available online from The Daily Beast (2010).

Yorzinski, J. L., and Platt, M. L. *Same-Sex Gaze Attraction Influences Mate-Choice Copying in Humans*, published online (2010).

Index